Liz

Body of Awareness:

A Somatic and Developmental Approach to Psychotherapy

Ruella Frank, Ph.D.

About The Author

Ruella Frank has a master's degree in movement education and a doctorate in somatic psychology. She practices psychotherapy in New York City, where she is the Director of the Center for Somatic Studies and a member of the training faculty at the New York Institute for Gestalt Therapy and the Gestalt Associates for Psychotherapy. Ruella also teaches at several institutes and universities throughout the United States and Europe.

Body of Awareness:

A Somatic and Developmental Approach to Psychotherapy

Ruella Frank, Ph.D.

Published by: GestaltPress
Distributed by: The Analytic Press

Published 2001
By GestaltPress

Published by GestaltPress, formerly GIC Press, 66 Orchard Street
Cambridge, Massachusetts 02140

Distributed by The Analytic Press, Inc., Hillsdale, New Jersey

A version of the chapter "Coming into Wholeness: Annie's Story"
appeared in *Studies in Gestalt Therapy*, No. 6/7, 1998/99.

The chapter "Reaching and Being Reached" was pre-published in
The Gestalt Review, Vol. 4 (4), 2000.

Library of Congress Cataloguing-in-Publication Data
ISBN 0-88163-347-X

First Printing

Cover design by Stacey Wyman

For David

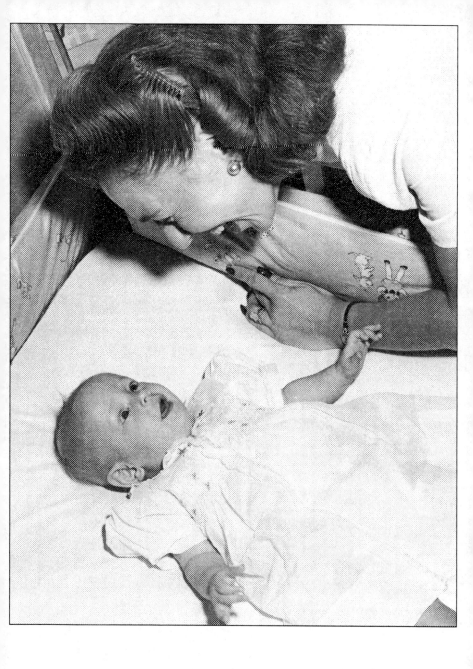

I see you see me.
In experiencing another, we experience ourselves.

Contents

Contents

A Tribute To My Teachers

The inspiration for this book has come from years of study with several wonderful teachers. They have deeply influenced my work and my life, and I wish to pay tribute to them here.

Laura Perls, one of the founders of Gestalt psychotherapy along with Fritz Perls and Paul Goodman, was a remarkable woman and a unique trailblazer. She had the ability to illuminate the most intricate of theoretical constructs with simplicity and ease, and demonstrated brilliantly the art of Gestalt therapy. With Laura as my model, I felt encouraged to explore the boundaries of Gestalt therapy theory and its practice.

Richard Kitzler, a founding member of the New York Institute for Gestalt Therapy and one of the world's leading Gestalt therapy theorists, imparted to me an appreciation of the richness of our unique theory and gave me a profound understanding of the wholeness of experience. He has been always generous with his knowledge and his time, and has served as a "wise advisor" to me in the developing of my ideas.

Bonnie Bainbridge Cohen, founder of the School for Body/Mind Centering, is an original thinker in her approach to movement analysis and movement re-education. Her understanding of the subtleties of human movement patterns taught me how to experience and express myself in depth and with clarity, and provided a springboard for my continuing explorations in somatic development. I also wish to acknowledge several of her teachers with whom I have studied: *Sandy Jamrog, Gail Stern,* and *Genny Kapuler.*

Esther Thelen is one of the leading researchers and theorists in the field of developmental psychology. Esther's innovative experiments with infants as well as her critical thinking have been significant in the formulating of my own concepts. Although I have not studied with her formally, I have benefited greatly from her writings.

All the teachers of the Iyengar Yoga Institute of New York, in particular, *Mary Dunn* and *Genny Kapuler,* have taught me the science and art of yoga and have opened me to a profound system of healing through movement.

For the gift of their teaching, I am truly grateful.

Acknowledgments

I wish to thank all my colleagues at the New York Institute for Gestalt Therapy for creating a unique atmosphere in which ongoing lively discussions of Gestalt theory are encouraged. They have taught me to be bold in my thinking and to stand up for my beliefs. I thank my fellow faculty members at the Gestalt Associates for Psychotherapy who have provided an environment in which I am free to experiment and further develop my teaching skills. I also wish to thank Carmen Vazquez Bandin and the students of the Centro de Terapia y Psicologia in Madrid for welcoming me into their training program so open-heartedly.

I am indebted to the Union Institute Graduate School for providing a setting that encouraged me to follow my passion. During my doctoral studies at the Union, I researched and began to develop the theoretical constructs upon which this book is based. Dr. Judith Arcana, who served as my core professor, was an early supporter of my interdisciplinary endeavors, and her abiding interest and encouragement have been deeply appreciated.

I thank my colleagues at the GestaltPress whose enthusiasm about the material was most welcome. In particular, I wish to thank Deborah Ullman for her valuable comments on the final manuscript and her efforts in bringing the book to publication. Several dear friends and colleagues provided a constant support as I struggled with the writing. Polly Howells and Eric Werthman offered their love and kindness whenever necessary, for which I am truly appreciative. Dan Bloom was always there to listen to my theoretical formulations, and shared his intelligence and wit as we engaged in wonderfully philosophical conversations at 8:00 a.m. almost every morning. Phil Lichtenberg read the first draft of every chapter and his comments were important and useful as was his gentle wisdom regarding the agonies of writing. Richard Kitzler spent hours commenting on every chapter and helping me clarify my concepts. Sara Blackburn read the final draft, and made suggestions so that the manuscript could "breathe."

I am grateful to my dear clients who have taught me the craft of psychotherapy. Without them, this book could not have been written. I am especially appreciative to those clients who have permitted me to tell their stories here. I also thank my students who have given me the opportunity to explore and refine my work as we continue to learn together.

My husband, David Johnson, has given his heart to this creative process since its inception and has been invaluable to the organizing of my work. His brilliant, analytic talents were put to good use as he edited every rough draft as well as thoroughly going over the final manuscript. He was always there to challenge my thinking and, in so doing, to support my efforts. More significantly, he has loved me.

Notes To The Reader

Disguising the Client: Although the historic material within each case study has been altered to disguise the client, the therapy session that unfolds is factual. These studies have been based on my detailed notations and later recollections. I selected those clients for each study that I believed would best illuminate the theoretical material discussed within the chapter. Most of the clients presented here are female. This was not intentional.

Issue of Gender: It can be a struggle for writers to decide upon the most appropriate singular pronoun when referring to a general population. Some writers opt for using "s/he," or "she/he," "his/hers," or even "they," "their," or "themselves." I have found these kinds of resolutions to be a burden as both a reader and a writer. And, the alternative usage of "he" to describe a general group simply does not work for me. When I read a sentence with he, and then reread it using the pronoun she, a different feeling and image are created within me. With that in mind, I have settled upon using the masculine pronoun "he" in some situations and the feminine pronoun "she" in others. Until our language "catches up" with our culture, this will have to suffice.

Introduction

One of the hallmarks of this twenty-first century is the interdisciplinary path many researchers and theorists have taken to further understand human experience. Presently, the developing field of psychology draws from neuroscience, biomechanics, dynamic systems theory, developmental embryology, various social sciences, and other disciplines. The resulting synthesis offers not only new knowledge, but new ways of looking at what already is known. This has been especially true in the area of human development, where sophisticated experimentation has given us deeper insight into the nature of the infant and experiences of early life. A major shift is taking place in our understanding of infant processes and the relationship between these early processes and adult experience. With this comes the inevitability for innovative models of psychotherapy.

With contemporary research generated within these separate but interrelating communities, I am now able to articulate more clearly why my work with psychotherapy clients has been effective, and to propose it as a template for other practitioners. The heart of my work is to examine movement experiences throughout development and to understand their contribution to the organizing self. It is based in my interests and background as a former professional dancer and choreographer, a practitioner of Gestalt psychotherapy, and a movement educator.

In the mid-1970s, Bonnie Bainbridge Cohen, the founder of the School for Body-Mind Centering, introduced me to the idea that when adults move in patterns similar to those of infants, they create substantial changes in their neuromuscular systems, developing greater strength and flexibility. So deep was my personal experience in exploring these patterns that I began to teach them to my bodywork clients, in movement classes, and workshops. Prior to this time, my focus was to heighten my clients'/students' sensorimotor awareness so that they could move more gracefully through the world, or become aware of what prevented them from doing so. It was no surprise that during sessions or in classes critical shifts in their experience occurred. Often the work elicited unexpected emotions for those who engaged in it and created authentic changes in the person's perceptions and attitudes. When we began to experiment with developmental movements, however, the psychological material that surfaced seemed far more intense and immediate, and more apparently relevant to the person's present concerns. I became fascinated by what my clients and I were seeing and feeling.

By the early 1980s, I was teaching developmental patterns to a group of Gestalt psychotherapy students and trainers and on several occasions had presented the work at their conferences. At one such conference, I was privileged to witness Laura Perls, creator of Gestalt therapy along with Fritz Perls and Paul Goodman, conduct a psychotherapy demonstration. Laura attended to her client's feet, and encouraged him to bend and straighten his knees until he clearly sensed his relation to the floor. The ease with which she integrated movement into the session showed me that Gestalt psychotherapy was beautifully holistic and that it was well suited to the kind of work I was developing.[1]

I began my own studies in Gestalt therapy a few years later. As my training progressed, I realized that the infant developmental patterns could be used to analyze every aspect of a client's movements—posture, changes in weight, gait, the gestures of all the body's parts—and further, that they could be incorporated into the session to heighten the client's awareness and to reorganize his or her experience.

In the fall of 1985, and after three years of Gestalt training, I read psychoanalyst Daniel Stern's classic work, "The Interpersonal World of the Human Infant." Rather than regarding development as occurring in discrete and linear phases, an assumption that was always disputed by the Gestalt therapy theorists, Stern proposed that an organizing of self emerges in overlapping waves and that it is dynamic in nature. Thus, an ongoing interaction with the past exists in all of our present experience. This was a process-oriented approach and as such in keeping with Gestalt therapy theory. Further, the developing *self* was now clearly seen as "interactive" from the very beginning. This solidified my understanding that the infant and caregiver influence each other and together co-organize the field.

Ten years later, and as I continued to hone my therapeutic skills, I discovered the work of developmental motor theorist Esther Thelen and her colleagues. Previous to Dr. Thelen's research and critical thinking, the field of motor development had become an almost extinct branch of developmental psychology. Maturation had been thought to be a process that is genetically driven. The nervous system was considered central to development, while the role of experience was relegated to a more peripheral position. Interest had shifted from motor activity to cognitive and social processes.

Dr. Thelen's novel research methods and findings brought the study of movement processes once again to the forefront of developmental psychology and with it, the primacy of experience. Thelen saw the experiences of infant perception and action—developmental patterns—as fundamental to the evolution of a child's mental and social life. It was evident to me that the infant movements I had been so taken with as a dancer and choreographer, and that were such a crucial part of my psychotherapy practice, were now assuming a prominent role in the study of human experience.

My challenge has been to integrate these infant movement patterns and the most recent research in human development with Gestalt therapy theory and practice. In my efforts to bring these dynamic strands together, a distinct approach to psychotherapy has emerged: one that makes lucidly evident the processes of early development as they continue to unfold in the present.

In this book, I explore the formation of infant movement experience and its manifest influence upon the later adult. Most significantly, I show how the organizing principles in early development are functionally equivalent to those of the adult. I demonstrate how movement plays a critical role in a developing self-awareness for the infant and in maintaining a healthy self throughout life. In addition, a variety of case studies illustrate how developmental movement patterns are part of the moment-to-moment processes of the adult client and how to bring these patterns to awareness within therapy. The client's emerging patterns of breathing, gesture, posture, and gait are understood from a developmental framework and attended to within the perspective of this somatic and developmental approach. The case studies convey how, through a variety of experiments, our movement patterns can be subtly altered to enrich rather than inhibit our current functioning.

Often psychotherapy students look for a book that tells them "what to do with the client." This is understandable for sitting with someone who relies on you for guidance, especially someone in great distress, arouses anxiety. Even advanced therapists experimenting in a new venue (for example, working with movement processes) sometimes wish for a repertory of ready techniques to use with their clients. Something too "theoretical" appears difficult to grasp. Yet something too full of examples may seem like a "how to manual." I hope I have blended the right proportion of practical illustrations within theory so that the reader understands with clarity how and why infant development is so critical to the psychotherapy process.

The success of any therapy is founded on the therapist's ability to attune to the client. It is essential for practitioners to let go of having to know *what to do* and attend instead to *what they see, and what they feel.* This book is intended to help therapists, new or advanced, to enhance their skills of attunement. They can do this by heightening their observations of subtle movement patterns as they emerge within the client/therapist field, and by respecting their own developing feelings within the session as essential information to the therapy process. And as developmental patterns are central to psychological functioning, a background study of movement provides the therapist with critical insight into the unfolding psychodynamic field.

Within each chapter, I have provided detailed physical descriptions of my clients whose histories have been carefully disguised. From these clear portraits, you will better sense the world of the client, as well as understand the phenomenological background out of which the prescribed therapy experiments arise. In addition, some basic anatomical and physiological information is supplied throughout the book to elucidate the physical processes of the infant and the adult. A certain amount of body science is essential for the therapist to become fluent in this approach.

Each therapist develops a unique style based on his or her personal history, individual talent, and training. Many of the experiments I demonstrate throughout the book—sitting on large gymnastic balls, lying on the floor in a fetal position, pressing hands or feet onto a wall—will not be consistent with everyone's style, nor should they be. And surely not all therapy clients feel comfortable, interested, or willing to experiment in the ways that I have illustrated. Nevertheless, with an understanding of the underlying theoretical constructs and a heightened ability to attune within the session, therapists will be able to create the somatic/developmental experiments that are best suited to themselves and their clients.

Finally, I have kept my use of Gestalt therapy terminology to a minimum within this book, although Gestalt is my practice and theoretical frame. I have chosen, instead, to explain these constructs through the "language of the body." By doing so, I expect to appeal to readers of various backgrounds and disciplines who have no understanding of Gestalt therapy theory and who could benefit by this approach. I hope that Gestalt psychotherapists will also appreciate the explication of complex theoretical concepts through this somatic and developmental vocabulary.

This book can be read in several different ways. It can be read, of course, from front to back. Or readers can begin with the final chapter, "Coming into Wholeness: Annie's Story," and then proceed to the first chapter and continue through the remainder of the book. In the latter approach, readers will be introduced to a full-length case study describing *what* I did with the client and *how* I did it. By reading the remainder of the book, they will come to understand *why* I did what I did. This is also true for chapters two to five where case studies toward the end of each chapter can be read prior to the foundation material supplied earlier.

A Brief Synopsis

Chapter One: Opening Dialogue

A client comes to her first therapy session with her three-and-a-half-month-old baby. The description of their nonverbal, moment-to-moment interactions vividly reveals how mother and infant influence and shape each other's experience. Through a heightened awareness of emerging patterns within the relational field, the mother comes to know her baby and herself. Their ongoing dialogue contributes to the formation of the infant's body— breathing, posture, gesture, gait—and sets the foundation for his style of contacting.

Chapter Two: Developmental Patterns and the Processes of Differentiation

Here we investigate the developmental movement patterns and their significant role in the infant's processes of differentiation. Every forming pattern is the infant's response within the relational field and underlies the progressive articulation of me and not-me. These patterns do not disappear after infancy; rather, they remain as part of the emerging and more highly organized processes of adult experience. Because earlier patterns integrate within later patterns to develop, all preceding patterns exist within the phenomenological present. We see how prior movement patterns provide the necessary, but in some cases not always sufficient, soil from which later patterns take root. A brief case study concludes the chapter and is used to demonstrate how developmental patterns serve as diagnosis and can be adapted for experiments within the adult session.

Chapter Three: Primary Orienting: Gravity, Earth, and Space

The sensing of our own movements, or proprioceptive awareness, organizes the primary orienting processes for both the infant and adult, and is experienced through our sensations of body weight. We observe here how the infant's experience of body weight forms a basic substratum of the emerging self. The background role of gravity, earth, and space in the organizing of the infant's yielding experience and falling reactions is explored. Detailed descriptions of two adult therapy clients illustrate how movement patterns express meaning and convey a fundamental sense of who we are and how we live within our worlds. Distortions in pattern reflect previous and unfinished experiences within an earlier relational field. Case studies show how experiments in yielding or falling are used within the therapy session to restore inhibited movement patterns, and to organize a more fluid orienting experience.

Chapter Four: Reaching and Being Reached

The reaching patterns of the infant, as mediated by the mouth, eyes, ears, and limbs take shape within the relational field. The functional similarities between infant and adult organizing processes are demonstrated through investigating the developing dynamics of reaching. A study of the rooting response (reaching with the mouth toward the nipple) details how infants function when they are receptive to the ongoing infant/caregiver dialogues. When receptivity is blocked, easy communicating is obstructed. Observing and experiencing reaching patterns provides a vital method for exploring the relational field for both therapist and client. The effectiveness of working with reaching gestures is seen through three case studies, as somatic/developmental experiments immediately elucidate the existential concerns of each client.

Chapter Five: The Upright Stance

This chapter explores the infant's progression toward verticality, as well as the relationship of upright experience to the psychological functioning of both infant and adult. Our upright expressions reveal how we have learned to support ourselves in the face of conflicting forces. The upright stance is the client's history as it manifests itself in the present. Two case studies illustrate how chronic interruptions in adult upright pattern express the incomplete experiences of an earlier relational field. Both clients are routinely unable to achieve and maintain a vertical alignment, which profoundly influences their behaviors. The somatic/developmental experiments used in the treatment of each provide the necessary underlying sensorimotor supports to gradually encourage their sense of *right*—a relation to the earth and in the world—their experience of authenticity.

Chapter Six: Coming into Wholeness: Annie's Story

Annie's story is narrated in this final chapter to demonstrate how developmental patterns work in concert within a long-term therapy. Annie was seriously damaged and functioning poorly when I first met her. The interweaving of somatic and developmental experiments throughout her therapy was crucial to our working through the blocks and obstructions that prevented her from living spontaneously and creatively. Several of her mystifying behaviors (important clues to her present experience) were clarified through an understanding of her somatic development. In addition, experimenting from a developmental framework enabled me to discover parts of Annie that could easily have been overlooked, crucial facets of her self that otherwise would not have been addressed. It becomes clear how experimenting with a diversity of developmental patterns offered a variety of relational experiences for both Annie and me. Annie's is an excellent example of therapy from a somatic and developmental perspective.

* * *

In writing this book, my wish has been to articulate through words what I am able to so easily articulate through the language of my body. At best, this is an uneasy task for those who write about somatic experience. I am no exception. I hope I have conveyed some of the joy I have experienced in locating and discovering the theoretical constructs woven throughout what follows, my love of the work as well as my conviction about its practical value.

Introduction Notes

1. Other Gestalt psychotherapists who have written about the role of physical processes within the therapy session and who have made important contributions to the field in general include Edward W. L. Smith (*The Body in Psychotherapy,* 1985) and James Kepner (*Body Process: A Gestalt Approach to Working with the Body in Psychotherapy, 1987*).

Chapter One

ॐ

Opening Dialogue

I want to begin at the beginning by describing an infant/caregiver relationship as it emerged within the therapy session, a vignette that sets the background for the model of psychotherapy I advance. While seeing both an infant and a mother in therapy is not necessarily typical of my work, this narrative illustrates the powerful, nonverbal patterns by which infant and caregiver communicate.

All infants move through a similar sequence of patterns throughout their development, but each infant performs them differently and demonstrates his or her unique relationship to the caregiving environment. Vital information regarding infants' psychic lives is revealed through their movement patterns. The patterns are not *of* the infant, nor *of* the environment, but *of the relational field*. It is within the context of these interactions, that the infant forms: breathing, gesture, posture, and gait, all further informing the relationship.

Close observation of infants' movements offers us critical ground for understanding the adults they become. When psychotherapists use a somatic and developmental frame of reference within the session, we become sensitized to the emerging nonverbal dialogue within the therapy field, as well as to the background events that constitute the present moment. From this perspective we can more fully understand what we see and what we feel.

As you familiarize yourself with the infant/caregiver dyad below, imagine the infant this mother once was, and the adult this infant will become.

The Emerging Dyad: Rachel and Alex

Rachel called to set an appointment for our first session. Unsure of whether she could find child care for our arranged time, she asked if she could bring Alex, her three-and-a-half-month-old baby. Working with a parent and infant is not unusual for me, and I have occasionally asked my clients to bring their babies to the session. When clients are in the process of caring for their children, unresolved issues from their own history generally emerge and become illuminated. The new baby offers parents an opportunity to work through the unfinished experiences of their childhoods. In the newly organizing relationship, many feelings may unravel: inadequacy ("I'm not good enough to take care of you"), sadness ("I wish someone had loved me the way I love you"), anger ("No one was there for me, why should I be there for you?"), desperation ("No matter what I do, you won't really love me"), terror ("In loving you, I could lose myself"). Such infant/caregiver dilemmas may be organized around particular areas of child-rearing tasks: feeding, sleeping, discipline, or comforting the child, and they are experienced and expressed through dialogical steps within the dyad.

The manner by which infants interchange nonverbally with their caregivers unfolds dynamically, organizing a *developmental, relational body-language.* Both partners influence and shape the other's experience. In concert with a genetic predisposition and the environment of the mother's womb, the developing body-language underlies the infant's relational style in the infant/caregiver field. The primary dialogic experiences are internalized setting a foundation for later relationships. A framework is created for how the child, the adolescent, and the later adult will support him or herself.

With my clients and their infants, I am privy to moments of spontaneous, creative exchanges as well as those moments when the dialogue between them becomes stuck, mutuality and receptivity impaired. Formerly smooth, nonverbal interactions become poorly coordinated and awkward. The newly forming body of the infant *and* the body of the caregiver visibly demonstrate the breach in communication. Each becomes anxious. When I observe their gestures, postures, and breathing patterns, I gain significant information.

For all these reasons, I welcomed getting to know Rachel by spending time with both her and the baby. I wondered if she sensed that she needed me to meet Alex, who was her first child. Encountering a new client and her baby at a *first* session would be a new experience for me.

The First Session

I opened the office door to greet Rachel, a tall, thin, attractive woman in her late thirties. When she removed her jacket, I noted that her head drooped forward, that the round of her shoulders created a depression at her collarbones, and that her upper chest was collapsed. Auburn hair framed Rachel's pale, translucent skin and delicate features, completing an overall look of fragility. For a moment, we exchanged hellos, and a broad, full smile erased her observable exhaustion.

She was carrying Alex, who was reclining in his plastic car seat. His face was round, cheeks rosey and ample. Removing the cotton blanket lying over him, I saw the fullness of his face restated in his body. Alex kicked excitedly and pushed his legs against my hands. His kick was strong and determined. While his mother lifted him out of his seat, I spread the cotton blanket on my office floor, and Rachel lay Alex onto his back.

They spent some moments playing, each one charmed with and completely absorbed by the other. I took several deep breaths and settled comfortably into my chair. When the baby was well-situated on the floor, a stuffed animal in hand, I gave my attention to Rachel who now sat in the chair across from me. Having worked with another therapist several years earlier, she was returning to therapy to "get some help," she said, while going through "all the overwhelming changes of the past few years:" falling in love, finding herself pregnant, getting married, giving birth to their son. "A lot has changed in a very short time. I feel so different," she said. A forced smile and sad, tired eyes accompanied Rachel's story. Every few sentences, she lifted her compressed upper torso, sharply inhaled and held onto her breath for a moment, then sighed aloud as she collapsed her rib cage once more. I felt with her on the brink of depletion and despair.

Rachel continued: "I used to be someone with rigid opinions and beliefs. Now I'm not sure about anything." Having made this statement, she moved her torso forward and over her legs, placed an elbow on each knee, turned her hands upward, and rested her weary head on them. Her ambivalent feelings, organized primarily around Alex, appeared to be weighing her down. She was unsure, she said, whether he should continue on breast-milk or begin formula, sleep in the bed with his parents or by himself in a crib. She felt pressured to make these decisions, and yet was completely confused: "I don't know what's best for him!" she pleaded, looking at me with soft, sad eyes.

Ten minutes into our meeting, Alex attempted to roll onto his left side. Rachel and I watched with fascination. Rotating from back to side generally requires that the infant push one foot, from heel to ball, onto the floor, which would extend the same-side knee, hip, and spine. Pushing the foot down, looking, and reaching with the same-side arm, shifts the infant's body weight in the direction of the roll; usually he is able to complete the movement with the assistance of gravity.

Instead of using his foot as leverage, Alex employed the strength of his back muscles to facilitate the rolling movement. Without the requisite push of his foot, and/or an energetic reach of his arm, he was not able to integrate the muscles along the front (flexors) and back (extensors) of his body to complete his exploration. Rolling was new for him, and all parts of the pattern did not yet cooperate, nor smoothly coordinate to create the whole.

What had begun as a playful activity soon became increasingly frustrating for Alex. He arched and extended his spine, and reached out with his hand, but he could not roll. I sat down next to the side toward which he was rolling and extended my hand to him. He tightly grasped my index and middle fingers. I held firmly, offering resistance, leverage and support. Alex pulled on my fingers with great effort. The pulling movement activated his abdominal muscles, and after several tugs, he was able to roll onto his side.

Alex was now extremely agitated. Even when he had accomplished the movement, he seemed to take no pleasure in having learned the activity. He cried, then wailed, and appeared unable to contend with either of these feelings. Rachel immediately picked him up and tried to console him, but Alex became progressively more distressed. His eyes shut tight as he cried. "He often cries with his eyes slammed shut," Rachel said. "The only way I can calm him down is to find interesting things for him to look at. That comforts him." Alex's head pressed forward, his neck tensed, his shoulders elevated, and his hands clenched.

For the rest of the hour, Rachel held Alex in her arms and faced him outward. The more distressed he became, the slower and more languid were Rachel's movements. "Alex, see the flowers, aren't they pretty? Oh, the pillows look so inviting. Look at the little cups." Her breathing constricted and her soft voice retreated into her throat, lifeless. Although clearly devoted to caring for her baby, she was collapsing, becoming remote, and apparently closing herself off from experience. I sensed my own chest and abdomen tense, felt my breathing constrict, and noticed a growing frustration.

Now Alex opened his eyes, shifted his head sharply, and moved his attention rapidly from one object to another. He seemed hungry to take in as much of the world as he could. Curious and distracted, he calmed. Then, as if from nowhere, he startled again and came undone. Wailing with enormous distress and seeming frustration, he held his body tight. He appeared incapable of taking comfort from his mother and powerless to soothe himself.

In a short time, I had learned how communication looked when Rachael and Alex had opened to and flowed with each other in an almost seamless fashion, and how each had closed off, ending the spontaneity of creative dialogue. When they were exploring, each of them seemed new and endlessly fascinating to the other and I absorbed the *whole* of their dynamic. My eyes moved effortlessly from one to another, my breathing was easy, and I felt relaxed. As I observed the moments of their disrupted and anxious connecting, my eyes were drawn to the *part* of each of their bodies that demonstrated the interruption: Alex's clutched hands and tense shoulders, his eyes slammed shut, or Rachel's chest, collapsing as she exhaled. Each of their movements, whether fluid or rigid, was a product of their dynamic interchange.

I attended to the emerging bodily patterns of each partner—exchanges of glances, reaches toward or away from one another, the changing qualities of their muscle tone, the rhythm of their breathing—as well as to my own experience, and diagnosed their ongoing relationship. It was not that Rachel was *doing something* to Alex, or that he was *doing something* to her to create their mutual distress. It was clear that both were vital members of an organizing field.

Rachel offered Alex her breast, sensing that he was hungry. While he nursed, I noticed that she was not supporting him sufficiently under his head or buttocks. Rather than curling him inward, and molding his body into hers, Rachel lay him in her lap with much of his belly facing upward and exposed. To find her nipple, he had to rotate his head almost completely toward her breast. As Alex strained to nurse, he could not rest easily into his mother's arms. Finally latching onto her breast, he sucked with such ferocity that he soon started choking and coughing. His eyes looked confused, frightened, and he cried. Rachel patted his back, and when his coughing subsided, she resumed nursing him. As if starved, Alex again sucked with all his might, choked, coughed, and then sobbed inconsolably. "This happens at almost every feeding," Rachel said. "I'm not sure why. He gobbles at my breast and chokes." She vocalized her deep sigh and sank back into the chair.

While I noted their newly forming partnership through primarily nonverbal interactions—breathing, posture, gestures—I witnessed how creativity was being rapidly replaced by habitual encounters that were no longer dynamic, no longer lively. For both Rachel and Alex, the dialogue between them too often created agitation, exhaustion and the dulled existence of routine. The possibilities for novel, spontaneous exchanges became blocked. The dyad was beginning to lose flexibility.

I also had noticed how stressed Alex looked when he was making a transition from one event to another: rolling from his back to his side; shifting his focus from one object to another; moving into and out of nursing. Finishing one activity and transferring attention to the next requires interest and curiosity. Alex's transitions seemed to be filled with persistent anxiety.

I asked Rachel if she felt that Alex had difficulty moving from wakefulness to sleep, sleeping to waking, playing to nursing, or in being placed down or picked up. Her eyes brightened, her spine lengthened, and she became more animated. "Yes, going from one thing to another is really difficult for him, especially waking up or going to sleep. Sleeping is a real struggle." I said that Alex appeared very sensitive to stimulation whether from *inside* himself or from the *external* environment. As we both had seen, he also had difficulty when he was frustrated, and he coped in ways that were routine and habitual: cried, wailed, and was unable to accept comfort from Rachel and/or to soothe himself. Further, Alex's lack of flexibility and resiliency in the face of new, developmental tasks was accompanied by his distressed and preemptory attempts to withdraw— "slamming" his eyes shut to cut out stimulation, clenching his shoulders, and fisting his hands. Within his newly expanding environment, Alex was having difficulty adjusting.

"A friend of mine told me he was difficult," Rachel revealed; "I wasn't sure what she meant." "He's not a difficult baby," I said. "He's having a difficult time." Rachel seemed interested in this.

Although Rachel could see when and how Alex struggled, she did not realize that his upset was exceptional. Not all babies experience the kind of agitation and disturbance that was rapidly becoming background to his development.

"Was *your* early life filled with chaos and confusion?" I wondered aloud. "Yes, my family had dramatic emotions," she said. "Everyone felt *something* all the time. And of course they let you know exactly what that was. Alex fits right in."

"What was that like for you?" I asked.

"I think I felt sad . . . all the time." Rachel disclosed, "Alex's dad used a lot of drugs. He's been straight for years now, but it took a long time for him to be able to deal with his feelings. He's still not great at it."

When our session was over, Rachel gathered a struggling Alex and placed him into his car seat. "He'll be fine once I'm walking with him. He loves movement. And, by the way," she added, "I can't always find a babysitter for him. If it's okay with you, I may have to bring him with me every few weeks."

"Sure. That will be a grand experiment," I replied.

Once Rachel and Alex had left, I collapsed into the big green armchair, exhausted and feeling empty. Were these my feelings, or had my body become a surrogate for the relational life of Rachel . . . or Alex . . . or both? I began feeling sad, as if some longed-for satisfaction had not been met.

Psychodynamics

I thought about my meeting with Alex and Rachel for several days. I knew that the reason for his behavior was not that he had been overtired, or had become overstimulated on that particular day. No, his display of behaviors in the session was normal for him, and a product of an often uneasy match with his mother.

While there were moments during the session when both infant and mother had been fascinated and captivated by one another, these were not long-lasting. Instead, Alex had dominated the hour with his misery and Rachel was unable to separate from his seemingly endless frustration; she was invariably trying to "fix" him, to make him feel better or to have an easier time. And the more frustrated he became, the more she appeared to lose herself: collapsing her spine, sighing and depleting herself of air, becoming remote. Even as he nursed, an experience that potentially can be loving and comforting to both parties, Alex's difficulties overshadowed the activity and consumed much of Rachael's attention. Apprehensive and unable to experience enough of herself in relation to him, she closed off. Her half of the potentially creative and fluid dialogue between them came to an abrupt halt.

Rachel sensed Alex's discomfort and her own exhaustion, but she did not identify these as unusual. The strain of relating to her son seemed to be characteristic of her routine way of life. She anxiously gave herself over to Alex, thereby losing the ability to differentiate herself clearly within the relationship. A casualty of her reaction to him, she relinquished a clear sense of self. I now understood the root dilemma that had brought Rachel to therapy.

Whatever happens in the world of the session indicates a client's experiences and behaviors within the greater environment. Rachel's pattern of relating to Alex was exemplary of her childhood, of how she related in the present, and of course, of her relationship with Alex's father, which was verified in later sessions.

Alex's difficulties were of a different nature. He seemed unable to cope with his anxious frustration, which readily developed, built rapidly to an intense level, and did not easily dissipate. The passion with which he ardently signaled for assistance was not met. He was inconsolable and at a loss to find relief. Even nursing at his mother's breast was arduous, confusing, and frightening. The ability to merge and flexibly separate from another person are requirements for any healthy dialogue. Rachel was unable to experience a necessary sense of separation in relation to her infant. Alex was unable to merge effortlessly with his mother and lose himself to her comforting arms. He anxiously withdrew and held tight, neither reaching toward her, nor nuzzling into her for solace. The experience of opening and closing, an ebb and flow in the process of relating, was losing its resiliency and becoming fixed.

Session Two: A Week Later

Rachel and I spent much of our second meeting processing what had happened with her and Alex during the previous week. I described for her the differences between the quality of her energetic expressions and those of her baby: "Alex moves with great determination, and uses as much effort as he can muster to accomplish his tasks. His style is robust, and his movements are highly energetic, quick and forceful. When he pressed into me, I really felt him. On the other hand, your style is slower than his. Your movements are softer, and executed with less vigor; your touch is lighter." "Alex is a lot like his father," she replied with a nervous smile. "They are both sweet, but a lot to deal with."

At the first session, I had observed Alex using the muscles of his back to pull himself over and onto his side, while his belly muscles appeared less strong and, therefore, unavailable. This pattern was exacerbated by the way Rachel positioned him while he nursed, his belly exposed rather than pressing into his mother's body. In addition, Rachel agreed that when Alex was distressed, he seemed to prefer to be faced outward and looking at objects rather than to snuggle into his mother for comfort. I asked her how Alex experienced lying on his belly. "He hates that position. He cries if I put him there," she said. [1]

I explained that the flexor muscles along the front of the torso are stimulated when the baby is placed belly down. When they are activated, these muscles bring the infant (child, adult) inward, with all parts of the body moving toward the center to withdraw, or protect. When the infant rests on his back, the extensor muscles are stimulated. These muscles bring the infant (child, adult) out and into the world. A harmonious relationship between the muscle tone of flexors and extensors creates the psycho-physical balance between extending into the world and returning to body/self.

For Alex, a pattern of extending had become preferable and associated with relative comfort. Molding into his mother's body and away from the world had not. Although the emerging flexor/extensor imbalance did not indicate neurologic problems or delays, it was enough to create difficulties in Alex's capacity to withdraw from stimulation, to produce disturbances in his sleep/wake cycles, and to contribute to his generalized irritability.

When I shared my observations with Rachel, she felt relieved. Her eyes appeared teary. "Maybe there's something I can do to help him feel easier," she said. I identified and validated her difficulties with Alex and suggested how she could become more effective in caring for him. I proposed several alternative ways she might nurse, carry, and play with him. Interested and excited by my suggestions, Rachel sighed. "If Alex has an easier time, maybe I could feel less exhausted," she said. Now Rachel began to reveal the intricate relationship between her caregiving experiences with Alex and the distress that drew her to therapy. "How do you feel when Alex cries and seems inconsolable?" I asked.

"Oh, I get really nervous. Sometimes I can't bear his pain. Sometimes I get angry, and then depressed." Rachel related a bedtime scenario of the night before. She had been sitting in her rocking chair with Alex on her lap, and was attempting to rock him to sleep. Although he was desperately tired, Alex arched his back into her arms as if to say "no" to sleep. As he protested, Rachel felt anxious and pulled away, aware of becoming cold and distant. "No, not again," she'd thought, "I can't take care of you. *I* need someone to take care of *me*."

Rachel's eyes filled with tears as she spoke. "You look sad," I said.

"Yes," was her reply.

"Where in your body do you experience your sadness?"

"My chest is heavy, weighted down. I feel sad right here." She placed her hand on her breastbone. I invited her to sense her hand on her chest, and to inhale and exhale easily. "Breathe, feel your sadness *and* your hand resting on your chest." With the support of her breath, and her hand placed on her chest, Rachel sobbed. When her crying was through, I asked, "Is this a familiar feeling for you?"

"Yes. I spent a lot of my childhood feeling this way." She continued, "My mother was very anxious, and when she was upset, she would withdraw from me. I remember her being upset a lot. Now I do that to Alex."

The unfinished experiences of Rachel's earlier environment, her relational past, now revealed within our therapy session, were being enacted with her own child. Although she loved him dearly, and with all the best intentions, the depth of her childhood wounds was crippling her ability to meet Alex openly and spontaneously.

The Therapy

Through therapy, Rachel became aware of the moments when she withdrew anxiously and abruptly, leaving Alex without the necessary support. At these times his anxiety would build to fitful disorganization. Further, she was able to notice when her anxiety pushed her to intervene prematurely, not wishing him to experience the emptiness and disappointment she knew so well herself. I told her that in either case, not intervening when the infant needs assistance, or intervening too soon, the child does not learn the rhythms of his mounting distress, nor does he learn to mobilize his efforts to reach toward the other, or when necessary, to soothe himself. Rachel seemed unable to allow Alex to develop his own resources and to discover what he needed to do to gratify himself. He was learning to be ineffectual. Because he was unable to influence her, he could not easily adjust within his expanding environment.

Although they had very different styles and expressions, Rachel and Alex shared a similar experience, debilitating powerlessness. While she was collapsing and giving in to hers, he was fighting his.

The therapy interventions created for both Rachel and Alex were based on my understanding of somatic/developmental patterns and their relationship to emergent psychological functioning. For example, I showed Rachel how to gather Alex together when lifting him by bringing his knees toward his belly and his arms toward his chest, and in the direction of his knees. Folding Alex inward would heighten his awareness of his abdominal muscles through the mild stimulation the action produced. It would also limit his extensor movements and give him the sense of containment. I also demonstrated how Rachel could sit on the floor, place Alex belly down across her thighs, and play with him. This would continue to heighten awareness of his belly, and help him tolerate spending more time in the prone position.

In addition, I showed Rachel how she could hold Alex's head and buttock area and nestle him into her body while nursing. To illustrate and help her experience what she would be giving him, I asked her permission to touch the back of her head. When she agreed, I placed my hand firmly where the back of her head joins the base of her skull and invited her to rest her head into my hand. Once she could feel the weight of her head gently releasing into my hand, Rachel understood the necessity of solid support. Now, Alex could easily rest into her arms and become more aware of himself. He could experience his gradually building anxiety, and learn to tolerate and contain the feeling. Unless he could do this, Alex's anxious moments would remain disruptive and disorganizing; attempts to regulate *internal* and *external* stimulations would continue to be highly stressful; and his experiencing and modulating emotions as they emerged throughout his infancy and childhood would continue to be perplexing.

In similar fashion, I designed a series of ongoing experiments based on infant somatic/developmental patterns to heighten Rachel's awareness of her body and behaviors. I had observed Rachel collapse and fold inward during significant moments of our sessions and I realized that this was her habitual expression. To heighten her awareness, I invited her to lie on the floor and experience an almost fetal position. To curl inward was soothing to her, she found, and preferable to extending her spine. Although folding into herself was her habitual refuge, she realized that she collapsed even more when she was anxious. It was her way to elicit compassion and signal that she needed help. Sadly, it had become a gesture that was made without awareness so that Rachel was left continually asking for assistance and resentful that it never came. Anxious, and unable to find someone to "fix" her, she had compensated for her loss by becoming acutely sensitive to anyone whom she perceived as needing "fixing," especially Alex.

Rachel also now experimented by extending and lengthening her body while she was sitting or standing. She found that when she expanded her spine, she became deeply disturbed. A profound confusion and upset surfaced, for if she stood upright and held her own, then "Who would hold me?" From the depths of her confusion, she slowly untangled the historic relationships that she had embodied and that were central to her present experience.

By our working with developmental patterns throughout her therapy, Rachel's awareness of bodily sensations deepened; she reorganized her capacity to experience and express her emotions; she expanded her repertoire of being and behaving. A familiar cloud of disorientation lifted, and she slowly relinquished the victim experience. More and more Rachel is present, effectual. She is able to live a more differentiated sense of *self* within the dialogic process. And Alex is learning to become a presence in the world, one who can influence others and alter his own experience. Rachel *and* Alex emerge.

*　*　*

In the following chapters, the developing somatic and relational patterns that enabled Alex to experience himself and his world are discussed in detail. Case vignettes demonstrate how these patterns are available and can be stimulated within the adult client to heighten awareness and illuminate the tasks of therapy. Using this approach, therapists will understand how to work with the primary and fundamental interruptions in their clients' sensations, emotions, perceptions, and behavior as these emerge in the phenomenological present. As the vignettes unfold, it will be seen that the functional similarities, if not identities, between the infant and adult have broad implications for the processes of psychotherapy.

Chapter One Notes
Opening Dialogue

1. Following the advice of her pediatrician, Rachel never allowed Alex to sleep on his belly in order to ensure against Sudden Infant Death Syndrome (SIDS), thought to occur when young infants who are lying on their bellies attempt to move their heads from one side to the other and suffocate in the process. Although the syndrome is not well understood, much of the medical community advises that SIDS can be prevented by placing infants on their backs when sleeping.

Chapter Two

ℰ

Developmental Patterns
and the
Processes of Differentiation

As a practitioner of a process-oriented, experiential psychotherapy, I must understand *how* my clients organize their experience; how they create their perceptions and emotions; beliefs and desires; thoughts and attitudes; and how they find gratification, or cope when satisfaction is lacking. The sum total of clients' organizing processes as well as their potential for change exists within the present moment of the session. I focus my attention on the ongoing phenomena that emerge within the therapy dyad, and shape interventions that directly address each client's individual organizing style. It is through a heightening awareness in the here and now that change at the most rudimentary level of functioning is made possible. When central nervous system processes shift, a healthy aggressive energy is freed. The client is able to function more spontaneously and creatively in his or her everyday existence.

I have found that the most direct method of discovering how clients organize their experience is by observing their movement patterns. Our movements are organized in terms of rhythmic contractions and releases. Muscles pull bones either away from or toward the body's center. These recurring patterns of compression and expansion express an intention to move toward what is inviting and appealing, or to pull back and retreat from what is not.

Attending to movement is especially powerful when it is guided by developmental theory. Although working somatically as a way to promote change is certainly not new to the world of psychotherapy, an awareness of movement patterns within a developmental context offers new and broad insights in both diagnosis and treatment.

The patterns by which infants tackle or overcome obstacles in the service of satisfying their curiosities, interests, and needs are the kinetic processes by which they grow. Throughout the developing life-span, infant to adult, fluidly forming patterns of movement serve as the basis for healthy autonomy. One requirement of autonomous functioning is that individuals acquire the capacity to differentiate themselves from the other, as well as the capacity to relinquish their separateness and merge. This fluidity of boundaries establishes a stable and secure sense of self, one that has the ability to encounter obstacles and find solutions, all the while flexibly choosing for oneself.

This chapter presents the foundation for all movements, the developmental patterns, and explores their crucial role in the processes of differentiation, as well as their function as underlying supports for all experience. Case vignettes are presented to illustrate how these patterns are used in diagnosis and adapted for treatment within the therapy session.

Contacting and the Emergence of Pattern

Beginning in the womb and emerging throughout the first years of life, developmental movement patterns facilitate the earliest formation of self-perception and other perception, self-knowing and discovery of the other. In this way, developmental movements underlie the progressive articulation of me and not me. The patterns are evident in the very visible leaps in function that we experience: sucking to chewing; creeping on our hands and knees to standing; standing to toddling; and toddling to walking. These movement milestones accompany and propel the continuous processes of differentiation. Developmental patterns enable infants to become increasingly autonomous, separating from while including the other in their experience. It is through evolving patterns that infants learn about themselves and their world. *All other learning emerges as an outgrowth or elaboration of these early organizing experiences.*

Every forming pattern is a primary response to the relational environment and expresses a dominant need at the time of its emergence. Each pattern promotes the processes of *contacting*, the quality and style by which infants (and children, adolescents, adults) are continually *in touch with* their bodies and the proximal environment.[1] As a need arises, stirred from within the inner or outer environment, the infant moves toward or away from the other in an attempt to find satisfaction. A two-month-old reaches with his mouth toward the nipple (breast or bottle). The need accompanying the emergent reaching pattern may be the infant's stirring of hunger or a need for comfort. The odor of the milk and the warmth of the caregiver's body also contribute to the infant's hungry sensations and desire for comfort. He explores the nipple with his mouth and becomes aware of its distinct properties.[2] In the experience of sucking, the infant is absorbed with the caregiver, and the caregiver, in turn, is involved with the infant, as is evident in their mutual gazing.

When the infant feels nourished and satisfied, the movement toward the object of interest is completed, and the infant withdraws and rests. The withdrawal provides a transition during which the infant assimilates the physical/social event, and the act completes itself. Now the infant's attention and energy are free to pour into the next fascination that moves him, the subsequent emerging curiosity. The fluid sequences of contacting continue. Every action brings with it newly forming psychic impressions of the world and novel experiences of the self in relationship to it. Through a repetition of such contacting episodes, and with as much awareness as is developmentally possible, the infant discovers the differences between me and not-me. He grows more capable of spontaneously and creatively adjusting within the absorbing environment.

As developmental patterns unfold, they organize dynamically through space and in time. Each pattern is *self-organized.*[3] As infants investigate their environments, they select the best means by which to explore. The movement patterns that emerge within the relational field are simply the most obvious resolutions among the possible choices of any situation and involve the coordination of several factors. These factors include the infant's present capabilities—muscle strength, biomechanical abilities, cognitive faculties, the infant's prior history, and present intentions—*and* the possibilities within the caregiving environment. When a pattern such as crawling comes into being, it is always a function of an organism/environment relationship. It is a field event and cannot be separated out as *of* the infant or *of* the environment. Because of this mutual, reciprocal, and interactive nature of the patterns, the infant molds to the environment, and the environment—primarily the caregiver—molds to the infant. For each infant, this creates an enormous variety in the form and function of every developmental pattern.

During the first year and as the infant's psycho-physical capacity grows, the field matures. When current patterns are no longer useful in the changing organism/environment field, they disorganize. Earlier patterns become others that are more adaptive to the advancing psycho-physical organization. Sucking as a mode of eating becomes obsolete when teeth are there to offer an alternative. And crawling is less preferable once toddling or walking becomes an enjoyable possibility for locomotion.

These earlier patterns do not disappear in the infant. Instead they remain part/whole of the emerging and more highly organized processes. They integrate within those patterns that are newly achieved[4] and serve other functions.[5] The coordination of lips, tongue, and jaw that makes reaching for the breast or bottle possible is also present and further developed in the act of forming words, and in the more sophisticated patterns of speech.

To better understand how the later developing pattern is always an outgrowth of the former, let us look at an example. A two-month-old swipes at objects with her arms and hands in an attempt to reach the other. As the muscles of her arms and hands are neither developed nor coordinated enough to initiate the movement, her reaching originates from the shoulder area. The infant experiences the weight of her arms as they carve a pathway through space and toward the object. She senses her arms as different from the rest of her body and from the environment. The stimulating object, whether person or thing, helps determine the movement's shape. It organizes the infant's intention, the movement's direction, and the required energy needed to accomplish the task.

Several months later and through many more reaching experiences, the infant's shoulder and arm muscles grow stronger and more stable in their respective sockets. The energy, shape, and flow of each preceding swipe influence the development of muscles, ligaments, and tendons which, in turn, determine the quality and direction of the following reach. With each practice, the shoulder, arm, and hand are further differentiated from each other and from the infant's torso. The process of reaching evolves into a more highly organized and coordinated pattern. This gives the infant greater control for both orienting and manipulating within the infant/environment field.

The later and more complex reaches from the arms, hands, and fingers are dependent upon the earlier and more basic patterns originating from the shoulder sockets. The sophisticated pattern relies on the preceding pattern for stability and flexibility. Development proceeds in this fashion. The earlier patterns become underlying supports for the later ones, and the infant becomes more fluent within the relational field. Similarly, how children stand and walk on two legs is consequent to how they moved on four limbs and previews hopping and skipping—later patterns that are to appear once walking is mastered.

In this way, developmental patterns in overlapping sequences become the foundation for all movement possibilities. They form the body of not only the infant, but the child, the adolescent, and the later adult. Each pattern contains within it the roots of the earlier motor experience and the seeds for the next function to emerge. Seen from this perspective, developmental movement patterns are like threads that weave throughout the fabric of our lives. Like breathing, they are perceptible, subtle, yet fundamental, and part of us since our origins.

Primary Supports for Contacting
and their Disruptions

As patterns form, integrate, and assimilate into the infant's developing nervous system, they become essential supports for contacting. This is not to say that supports and contacting are a duality, but they are inextricably linked and reciprocal in nature. Healthy contacting, whether infant or adult, relies on the adequate background support of these spontaneously emerging patterns, and the sensorimotor patterns are the system by which contacting eventuates. As more supports integrate and assimilate into the nervous system, a higher degree of organization takes place.

It was Laura Perls, one of the founders of Gestalt psychotherapy along with Fritz Perls and their colleague Paul Goodman, who first expressed the idea that coordinated movement patterns serve as primary supports for contacting. While she wrote only one book, *Living at the Boundary* (1992), in which this concept was briefly discussed, her therapy and teaching demonstrated her belief that sharp awareness of the differences between oneself and another, an essential component of contacting, always emerges from a background of primary supports.

In a general sense, this background of supports is that which is experienced as stable and secure so that an individual's curiosities, interests, and needs emerge with clarity. Adding the developmental dimension to this notion of support, it becomes clear how movement patterns spontaneously organize and provide flexibility for creative adjusting over time and how patterns organize in chronic disruption and produce fixation and maladjustment. Looking through a somatic developmental lens, the therapist understands how the client's movement patterns have emerged in infancy, and have adapted through time. This furthers the therapist's understanding of his or her client's organizing processes in the present.

For developmental patterns to emerge with grace, fluidity, and efficiency, infant and caregiver must be matched well enough, one to the other, so that the needs of each partner are met sufficiently enough of the time. This does not mean that every adjusting is smooth and easygoing, nor should it be. Within a field that is often filled with struggle and disappointment, infants learn to cope with many moments of not having their needs met. The caregiver must be available and attentive as much as is necessary for the infant to thrive, but not so much so that the healthy processes of development cannot proceed spontaneously.

Certain infant/caregiver matches become so chronically distressing that neither partner feels met nor satisfied as often as needed. Perhaps the caregiver looks to the infant to satisfy too many of her own needs. She may be overly attentive and therefore intrusive. The infant does not learn to resolve his dilemmas by exploring and discovering his own solutions, for he lacks the opportunity to draw on his own resources. Or the caregiver may be neglectful, and the infant must struggle with what is beyond his developmental scope. He may be asked to do what he is not mature enough to do. Overwhelmed, he loses himself in the process. In these relationships, often a combination of both styles of caregiving, the infant cannot creatively adjust within the dyad. He learns to adapt with hesitation and reluctance. Experiences of separating from and including the other become inhibited, and the meeting of one and another becomes fixed and routine, without grace.

The developmental patterns that emerge during the time of the disruption demonstrate this dysfunction. Contacting is thwarted. The poorly coordinated pattern is internalized and integrated into the nervous system of the child, meaning that it is made a part of the whole, but is not assimilated or taken into the system in a way that produces balance and harmony. That is, the discordant pattern will come to dominate the system, and to overpower the preceding pattern as well as the subsequent pattern that emerges.

A Closer Look at Differentiation: The Emergence of Toddling

With great enthusiasm, a ten-month-old infant pulls herself upright and begins to toddle. Her first steps are awkward and uncertain. Environmental possibilities expand in relation to her expanding potential. There is more to see, touch, and smell. The toddler both elicits and receives many new and different responses from her family. Some members are delighted at the child's new skills and the furtherance of her maturity. Others are overwhelmed with their inability to control the child, or sad for the loss of their infant's earlier dependency. The variety of environmental responses stimulates the child and becomes part of her toddling experience. Imagine the freely exploring body of an eighteen-month-old child whose family is elated at her newly acquired ability, as compared to what might be the more cautious expressions captured in the body of another child whose family responds with anxiety at the prospect of his every fall. Within a mutually regulating field, the body of the infant—posture, gestures, breathing and gait—takes shape.

The following scenarios depict two infant/caregiving dyads. While one field enables healthy and fluid contacting, the other hampers its possibility.

Toddling: In Spontaneity

For the toddler who experiences the environment as inviting and safe, explorations are without inhibition. She will fall, pick herself up, and retain her excitement as she meets the challenges posed by this major developmental task. Often enough, the caregiver is there creating an environment from which the necessary assistance is made available. The caregiver's presence, neither too active nor too passive, enables the child to discover and create the requisite energy for her upright explorations.

In the emergence of toddling, the infant shifts her weight from one foot to the other. At the same time, she maintains the balance of her head in relation to a now vertical spine. For a moment, precarious stability is discovered. Once equilibrium is found, and with the addition of two outstretched arms helping her to balance, she commits herself. The infant shifts her weight to one leg and reaches out with the other. In the act, the infant falls forward and to the side until the momentarily unweighted foot strikes the earth and catches the fall. The toddler inches her way through space in a forward-going, side-to-side trajectory. She spontaneously adjusts herself to the demands of the physical environment and in relation to her attending caregivers.

In this smooth forming pattern, movement flows from the periphery, the sense organs and limbs, and continues through the body. That is, the infant's eyes reach out and orient her in space, while one leg extends into the environment. In particular, the psoas muscles (originating at either side of the twelfth thoracic vertebra and inserting into the inner ridge of each upper thighbone) are the primary flexors used to move the legs. When the psoas muscle contracts, the inner thigh lifts and allows the leg to swing forward. As the extended leg reaches out and finds the support of the earth, an experience of weight travels up through the leg, into the pelvis and spine, and ripples upward to the head. Toddling is a whole body event. With practice, the energetic movement flowing from periphery/limb to core/spine gives infants an understanding of the relationship between the body's center and what exists at its boundaries. The infant differentiates between me and other.

The toddling pattern forms within the security and stability of the infant/caregiver field. When the infant is suddenly frightened, the pattern disorganizes momentarily. Once the child is comforted, it reorganizes and stabilizes again, and the child continues with his toddling adventures. The pattern is able to flexibly adjust, while retaining an integrity of the whole. In order for a pattern to assimilate into the developing nervous system, it must have the capacity to adjust flexibly within the field. It must disorganize and reorganize without losing a harmonious relationship to the whole. Thus, the uninhibited primary pattern, with its properties of flexibility and balance unimpaired, lends its support for contacting.

Toddling: In Disruption

For the infant who is tentative and apprehensive in his explorations, a far different pattern emerges. Imagine a scenario in which the caregiver suffers from an inability to trust the world as a safe place and an intolerable anxiety.

Whenever the infant explores, the caregiver fears for his safety. She surrounds him with her unwanted help and her hovering, uneasy presence. In response, the sensitive infant suppresses his curiosity and excitement. He temporarily holds his breath and retracts his arms, legs, and head into his torso. This creates further restriction at the surrounding joints and arrests a healthy and spontaneous outward aggression.

If these episodes continue, the toddler tightens his muscles and holds his breath in a habitual rebuttal to his caregiver's distress. The extensor muscles along the back tense, and in time, pull the psoas muscles along the front out of alignment. The psoas muscles no longer function efficiently to stabilize the spine nor initiate the pattern. Toddling loses a natural spontaneity and grace. The movement grows awkward, uncoordinated and inept. What was initially a temporary and creative adjustment ultimately becomes fixed and no longer spontaneous. When there are ongoing constrictions, the transitions from one movement to the next become difficult. Every toddling pattern thereafter builds on and reinforces the disrupted action.

Given the lack of lower-body stability, the upper extremities are called upon in an attempt to offset the strain. Compensations can be observed in neck tension, an elevation in the shoulder area, and an imbalance between the head and the spine. Later, the overuse of spinal extensor muscles will create a swayback as the pelvis is pulled out of alignment with both head and thorax. With such disruptions in the smooth flow between one part of the body and the other and in relation to the environment, connecting to the earth becomes increasingly unstable. The infant reaches out to a world that feels shaky and uncertain. This further reinforces the already awkward and cautious pattern.

When the natural sequence of movements habitually does not complete itself, the needs of the child are unmet and remain dissatisfied. Their ongoing demands are evident in the child's body and behaviors. He does not easily perceive one part of his body as separate from the other, or distinguish himself in clear relation to the environment. The ability to maintain a sharp awareness of the differences between himself and the other—the foundation for fluid, spontaneous contacting—is interrupted. If the environment remains routinely anxious throughout development, and/or the child does not grow more hardy in his capacity to adapt flexibly within a suppressing field, the disrupted pattern continues.

In such distress, the forming pattern influences and interferes with the emergence of the subsequent pattern, walking, and distorts the earlier pattern, standing. The inhibition in movement pattern reverberates at every level of functioning, as every emerging contacting episode lacks sufficient support. Compensations exist not only in the arena of muscular inhibition, but are also discovered in the reducing of sensory experience, in the inability to regulate emotions, and in the creating of strategies to avoid, reduce, and convert affect.

The Adult Psychotherapy Client

Just as the infant is always differentiating what is me and what is not within the caregiving dyad, so too does the adult continually articulate what is me and what is not within the therapy session. Much of the therapy assists the client in developing his or her capacity to differentiate within the client/therapist field.

Evaluation of the varied contacting experiences in the psychotherapy session is always based on aesthetic criteria that are observed and felt. In health, these criteria are made obvious by a lively vitality, an energetic flow, and a spontaneous, though at times, uneasy adjusting of one to another. In pathology, the aesthetic diminishes and there exists a lessening of liveliness, a reduction of excitation, and a chronic clumsiness in the ongoing formation of relationship. These criteria are most obvious in the observation of movement.

We experiential therapists continually evaluate contacting processes during therapy, and when we know how patterns emerge throughout early development, our assessment is greatly facilitated. A rotation of the ankle, a collapse of the spine, a misalignment of the jaw— all become important considerations for the evaluative processes in which we continually engage. Because earlier patterns become integrated within later ones, all preceding developmental movements exist within the phenomenological present. In this way, they are similar to past memories, regrets, and longings experienced and expressed in the here and now. In other words, the early organizing processes are manifest and accessible in the adult. As we therapists understand the inherent survival needs within each forming pattern, we are well advised as to *how* our clients organize in the present and in the presence of the therapist.

Simply put, the observation of somatic/developmental patterns allows the therapist a window into the experience of the client, while guiding him or her to an awareness of gesture, posture, breathing, gait. Developmental patterns not only alert both therapist and client to inhibitions in contacting supports, but can be adapted for experimentation. Such experiments in pattern enable more and more of the unexplored background to emerge into aware foreground experience. This includes all those experiences that would not have emerged as readily, as clearly, or, perhaps at all, without the investigation of pattern. What is revealed is the client's psychological organization, expressed through the primacy of movement.

Now, the chronically disruptive movement patterns, taken on initially as temporary assistance or compensations within an earlier field, become flexible and available for use. When inhibited support functions mobilize, carefully repressed or skillfully avoided emotions and perceptions are refreshed. Changes take place at a most rudimentary level, as will be seen in the following vignette.

Karla

When the processes of differentiation do not emerge flexibly, an awareness of the primary supports that are basic to maturation recedes more and more into the background, often irretrievably. To observe Karla's structure is to notice her diminished, essential supports for contacting. The parts of her body that are blotted out from her awareness manifest in a weakness of structural support. The weakness reflects visible difficulty in the emergence of movement pattern. Imitating or "trying on" Karla's patterns while reading these passages is a direct route to entering Karla's world, and to feeling empathy and compassion.

In this session, Karla reports that she has become more aware of her posture. When she was a child, her mother often admonished her to "stand-up-straight." The persistent remarks about her stature made Karla shrink. Now when she notices that she is slumping, she continues to feel "ashamed" and "bad about myself." I invite her to experiment and ask her to sit on a large (95cm.) red physioball.[6] The ball offers an enhanced support and allows Karla to better sense her body.

Sitting on the Ball

Karla's head pitches forward and up. In an effort to balance the weight of her head on her spine, her breastbone pulls backward. This creates the round of her upper back, and a lack of fullness in her chest. As if to hide, Karla's heart and lungs appear to press back and sink downward. The contraction leaves her unable to easily expand her lungs, and she is relegated to taking in mere teaspoons of air. Every so often, she lifts her shoulders and upper spine in order to pull in a more sufficient quantity of oxygen. Unaccustomed to feeling full here, she rapidly exhales what she has just taken in. Inadvertently, and yet chronically, she inhibits her every breath.

Karla's shoulder blades slide toward the sides of her rib cage and away from her backbone and the promise of stability. As each blade is connected to the outside edges of her collarbones, their sideward excursions press her collarbones forward in a pronounced fashion and make two hollows on either side of her upper breastbone. The sideward and forward movement of her shoulder blades forces the heads of her upper arm bones to roll inward in their sockets. At the same time, each arm bone thrusts subtly upward toward the direction of her ears. The opposition of Karla's organs moving down in the front and her muscles constricting upward in the back emphasizes her anxious and disheartened appearance.

Resting on the surface of the large ball, Karla's thigh bones roll outward so that her legs splay. Each bare foot balances on its outer edges, echoing the outward roll of her legs, and her soles face each other. With the compression of her head and upper spine pressing downward, and with no underlying and compensatory upward thrust from her feet, Karla's pelvis is unstable and rotates forward. The gesture exaggerates the natural arch of her lumbar spine. In summary, Karla's upper body collapses and intrudes into her pelvis. Her pelvic bowl, unable to bear the overload, dips forward and seems to spill its contents.

In what would appear as a complete contrast, Karla's eyes, lively and bright, signal an excitement within that has difficulty expressing itself. Her enthusiasm is also present in her vocal intonations, which have a varied quality and convey the capacity to invite.

The Therapy

I resonate with Karla's bodily expression, and feel the edge of a quickly developing exhaustion. I lengthen my spine and inhale deeply. Having considered my own experience, I ask Karla to attend to her body. We have worked together for almost two years, and Karla is now accustomed to these kinds of experiments. I ask her to exaggerate her habitual collapse. To heighten her awareness, I place my hand on her head and softly press downward. She follows the downward energy, compresses the bones of her neck and spine, and collapses even more into her pelvis. The adjustment further rounds her upper back and reinforces her dejected appearance. She reports, "I feel comfortable [*in this position.*]" It is a place to which she often retreats. The posture feels both natural and familiar and has become a kind of secondary physiology. I watch her and feel a pain in the small of my back.

I remove my hand and let it hover over Karla's head. Her spine rebounds as it recovers from its compressed state. I ask her to follow the lengthening impulse of her spine by pressing the soles of her feet into the floor, her tailbone into the ball, and reaching her head into my hand. With her lower body supports in place, Karla reaches upward. Her spine lengthens, and she shifts from her routine collapse to a more open position. She takes note of her experience and instantly becomes anxious. "I'm so big. I feel so exposed."

Again, I place my hand on her head and press downward. She follows my lead and compresses her spine. As she crumples downward, her anxiety dissipates. We do this several more times as she moves from a collapsed spine to an elongated one. Each time she executes this spinal movement, she becomes more flexible and receptive to her open posture. Her anxiety diminishes. Now Karla sits on the ball upright and balanced. "I feel an energy stream from my heart into my throat, out to my arms, and down into my pelvis," she says with enthusiasm.

I ask Karla to experiment further. "Align your knees directly over your toes, and press your feet onto the floor with even greater conviction." The press and release of her feet causes her to bounce on the ball. Her movements are joyous. I feel my excitement build. I move behind Karla and place my hands at the base of her skull. With a gentle lifting motion, I guide her head away from her neck. Her head and torso align. She continues to bounce. When she is finished, I ask her to stand and notice what she feels. Supported on two legs, her spine long and her chest open, she reports, "My feet are really solid and heavy on the earth, and I really feel my spine."

I stand in front of her and ask her to look at me. Again, her anxiety moves into the foreground. She begins to compress her new found postural pattern, and an early and familiar feeling emerges: if she exposes herself to me, I might criticize her. Now the structural fixation that accompanies her collapsed spine reveals itself, and the negative and introjected aspects of an earlier and unfinished situation become vivid. She quickly recognizes the parental dialogue of a former, yet persistent field. "It's not really you. It's my mother." She notices her stance. "Oh, I've collapsed again." "Yes," I say, "You've reduced yourself in my presence."

In response to my comment and with a more lively determination, Karla boldly stretches her spine to its full height.

I ask her permission to further experiment and to "try on" her posture myself. I reduce myself in her presence and feed back my authentic experience. This will allow her to experience the other side of the polarity: I am the one who shrinks, and she is the one who can be expansive and full. When I have deflated my lungs and compressed my spine, I look up at her. "I feel so small, and you are so big. I'm angry that you get to be so big and I'm stuck with being little."

Karla is struck by both my posture and my statement. "Do I look like that? Maybe I'm really angry too." She looks confused and disoriented. I ask her to exaggerate her length and pull her breastbone even further away from her pubis. She looks down at me and says, "I feel superior to you. That's a switch." She plays with her feelings of superiority for a while and then suggests that we exchange places. I grow in stature while she reduces herself. But she is now uncomfortable with a diminished self and she quickly positions herself between the extremes. "I'd like to be more equal," she states. "Yes, it would be a relief for both of us." I say. The session ends, but the experiment, just begun, will continue.

Several Weeks Later

Karla tells me about her difficulty in standing up for herself. Rather than disagree or conflict with her boyfriend, she is more likely to ignore her own needs and go along with his. This lack of assertion fits with her idea of being a "good person." She notices that she is slouching and deflated as she narrates her experience.

I ask if she would be willing to return to the previous postural experiment. She agrees. Standing, Karla easily and eagerly lengthens herself, assuming her full height. Again we explore the boundary between collapsing and feeling her fullness. This time she is able to accept the more open configuration and does not appear anxious. "Walk around the room and feel the length of your spine and your feet on the earth," I say.

In a natural and fluid gait, the weight shifts from both legs to one. The weighted leg pushes down and onto the earth and frees the unweighted leg. This leg reaches forward and out and places the heel of its foot onto the ground. The weight of the newly planted leg rolls from heel to the toe-ball and *pulls* back the earth. The pull propels the pelvis and torso forward. The body now rests on the pillar of this just-placed leg. The pulling motion has freed the back leg to reach forward, and the sequence repeats itself.

Karla's gait is tentative and ambivalent. I realize the inhibition in the reaching and pulling movements of her legs and feet. Each leg shuffles forward and her feet *plop* on the ground. To avoid rolling from the heel to the ball of each foot, she contracts the muscles of her shin and ankle, the very opposite of a healthy forward-going movement. This inhibits her trajectory and gives her gait an awkward and cautious appearance. Further conflicts are expressed in the area of her upper spine, pulling backward at the same time she reaches her leg forward. The tension of her spine inhibits the natural flow of her arms, which in a more flexible stride would move in opposition to the reaching and pulling of her legs.

I ask Karla to place her extended foot onto the ground and roll from the heel to the toe-ball. Once her weight has transferred to that foot, I ask her to push her toe-ball down and forcefully pull back the earth. Her walk now shifts, and she plows through space with healthy decisiveness. As she drives forward, her upper back loosens and moves more fluidly as do her arms. Although she enjoys herself, she says she is also anxious about the "consequences," of her aggressive stride. If she is "too bold," she will "overpower . . . maybe hurt someone." A fleeting look of disorientation appears on her face and she hesitates briefly. "You can always give up your pull," I suggest. Hearing this, Karla returns to her bold and valiant stride.

Psychodynamics

Karla routinely relinquishes her authentic sense of self. When she exposes who she is and what she wants, she fears she will be criticized. When her needs are different from someone else's, she feels frightened. If she is not who someone else wants her to be, she is convinced (and convincing) that she is hurtful, uncaring, even cruel. The loss of her self leaves her no choice but to become angry, an expression of separation. But for Karla, even her anger feels "too frightening," and is immediately converted into an anxious depression.

I observed Karla's movement pattern and noted the inhibition in support, her collapsed spine. To heighten her awareness of her collapse, I created an experiment based on the early infant's spinal pattern.

Spinal patterns are among the first to emerge as neonates develop neuromuscular strength and control from the center of their bodies to the periphery. A clarity in the emergence of spinal patterns enables the infant to differentiate between the head and the tailbone, the front and back of the torso, and to sense the relationship of interior to border. These patterns supply the strong central support for later movement explorations.[7]

Karla exaggerated her slouching position and explored her relation to space and the "very ground on which she stood." The compression experiment stimulated the sense receptors in the joints and muscles of her spine and attuned her to her experience. When any series of joints has been compressed and then is released, the surrounding muscles and ligaments respond directly by lengthening. Karla felt her spine subtly uncurl and followed the impulse by reaching her head upward. Our exploration in compression/extension movements stimulated her formerly inhibited spinal pattern into activity.

At the same time, the physical pattern carried with it the past, historic as well as future anxiety and discomfort. Suddenly, the conditions that accompanied Karla's slouching posture, as well as the attendant need to diminish herself, were illuminated. She felt anxious. I asked her to push both her feet onto the earth as an additional support for her novel upright expression, and the push onto the floor activated a kinetic chain from her feet, legs, thighs, and into her hip sockets. A more stable support for her pelvis and spine organized. As she pressed onto the floor, Karla bounced. The bouncing movement again stimulated a compression and elongation of her spinal column and enhanced her sensations.

Pushing patterns of the upper or lower extremities emanate from the hands or feet. They enable the differentiation of upper and lower halves of the body. The infant meets a resistant surface and exerts enough pressure to create a compactness of the body's surface tissues. He senses the support of the earth and is able to move through space. When the infant, on his belly, pushes from the lower limbs, he can move in the headward direction. Similarly, when the pushing movement originates from the upper limbs, he can move tailward. Pushing movements provide the necessary support for an upright posture in both the infant and the adult.

The pushing experiment stimulated a kinetic chain from the soles of Karla's feet upward and into her pelvis. The greater leverage from below enabled her to sense and find more length to her spine. In addition, she could further differentiate the periphery of her body (her feet) from her spine, and from the environment. Karla faced me, and again her anxiety emerged. With the greater supports available, however, she moved through her discomfort and could stand her ground.

At the post toddling period of the infant's development, a contralateral (meaning opposite-sided) reaching-and-pulling capacity emerges, emanating from the legs.[8] The reaching and then pulling movement of the foot allows the body to catapult through space to either advance toward what is interesting and compelling or pull back and away from what is uninviting and repellent. Without a clear pull, moving into or retreating from the environment is inhibited.

*   *   *

Karla's withdrawn posture served to sustain her primary relationships in an earlier environment, and provided a semblance of protection from a world that was habitually critical and shaming. In the present, it left her out of touch with both herself and others. An integration of developmental movement patterns into the therapy provided the incremental and necessary underlying supports to move Karla from her routine patterns to a more differentiated experience of self.

Chapter Two Notes
Developmental Patterns and the Processes of Differentiation

1. Contacting is a fundamental concept in Gestalt therapy theory and is further defined in F. Perls, R.F. Hefferline, and P. Goodman, *Gestalt Therapy: Excitement and Growth in the Human Personality* (London: reprinted by Guernsey Press, 1990).

2. A. N. Meltzoff and R.W. Borton, "Intermodal Matching by Human Neonates," *Nature* 282: 403-404.

3. Infants' self-organizing properties have been researched by developmental theorist Esther Thelen and colleagues (1984, 1987, 1989, 1992, 1993, 1995).

4. K. Bobath and B. Bobath, *Abnormal Postural Reflex Activity Caused by Brain Lesions* (London: William Heinemann Medical Books Limited, 1965).

5. P. Schilder, *Mind, Perception and Thought in their Constructive Aspects* (New York: Columbia University Press, 1947).

6. Physioballs are not the standard fare in psychotherapy. I use them, as well as a host of other such props, frequently in my work in order to heighten my clients awareness.

7. The concept and analysis of spinal patterns as well as the patterns of pushing, and reaching-and-pulling, were first introduced to me by Bonnie Bainbridge Cohen. They are part of a greater system of body analysis that is described in her book, *Sensing, Feeling, and Action* (1993).

8. When infants creep on their bellies or crawl on their hands and knees, the contralateral reaching-and-pulling capacity emanates from the upper extremities, the arms and hands.

Chapter Three

࿇

Primary Orienting Experience:
Gravity, Earth, and Space

Beginning therapy, people often express feeling out of control and victimized by their circumstances. They experience the environment as a force that is separate from themselves, something they must either act upon or be assaulted by. Underlying their sense of alienation is an incapacity to feel themselves as part of the larger surrounding environment. They also lack awareness of the inner environment that is their body. They are without the resources to inform themselves *that* they are, as well as *where* and *how* they are in relation to the other.

This distorted orientation is observed by the therapist and experienced by the client as inhibition in sensing, awkwardness in gesture and gait, distressed breathing, and distortions in postural configuration. In the realm of such bodily experience, these clients act and react in ways that persistently damage their sense of self. They feel estranged and become increasingly distressed. Left with only their imaginations, guesses, or projections to bridge the gap between themselves and their world, they attempt to validate their reality by desperately holding onto ideas about themselves as a replacement for more direct experiences. The less precise the experience of their bodies, the more they are compelled to rely on their constructed realities, routinely misinterpreting the presenting situation.

The work of therapy is to help clients organize their awareness so that they experience themselves as part of, rather than alienated from their environment. One of the first and most important therapeutic interventions with beginning clients is to ask *how* they sense themselves sitting on the chair, or *how* they sense the floor under their feet. These are inquiries of orienting.

For most clients, it is novel to know that the chair or the floor under and below them forms an integral part of their experience. Becoming aware of how these aspects of environment are taken in as part of their experience is crucial to the process of therapy, for the therapist as well as the client. Therapeutic experiments of primary orienting heighten awareness of the inextricable body/environment relationship, and restore the capacity for smooth, graceful, uninterrupted contacting. As clients broaden their awareness, they experience not only the actions that they will and plan, but all those acts of which they have been previously unaware. These range from the incessant tensions, aches and pains that accompany them daily and with no apparent cause, to behaviors and attitudes which they clearly do not experience, and therefore claim no responsibility for.

This chapter examines primary orienting through *proprioceptive awareness*, in particular, the awareness of body weight. It relates the developmental experiences that form infant sensations of weight to subsequent adult organizing processes. Case vignettes demonstrate the use of somatic/developmental experiments to significantly heighten awareness and enhance the orienting capacities of two adult clients.

Proprioceptive awareness is the sensing of our own movements. Along with our *external* senses, proprioception guides our responses in the world and underlies our capacity for orientation. Proprioceptive awareness develops in the womb as the fetus adjusts to uterine conditions during gestation and in preparation for birth. As the infant progresses, a developing proprioceptive awareness determines his or her ability to respond and relate within the environment. How infants experience their moving bodies forms the substratum for the emerging self, the responsive and continual engaging of infant and environment.

Throughout the life-span, from infancy to adulthood, proprioception encompasses all aspects of movement and includes: *kinesthetic*—a sense of movement, active or passive, and a sense of weight, resistances to movement or weight, and the relative positions of the body in relation to itself or the environment; *vestibular*—spatial awareness or sensitivity to the position of the head and body in relation to the earth, and direction of motion in space; and *visceral*—a sensitivity to pulsations of internal organs expressing levels of excitation and fatigue.[1] Although proprioceptive sensations are generally not experienced in awareness, they form the ground from which aware contacting emerges. In particular, it is the integration of kinesthetic and vestibular sensations that gives us our moment-to-moment information regarding where we are—our existence on the earth—and how we can move elsewhere—our relation to space and time. All these are aspects of orienting and organize in relation to the experience of weight.

Orienting Through Weight

We experience body weight in relation to gravity while resting on the earth, or in resisting gravity while moving through space. An awareness of such body weight sensations characterizes our receptivity to experience. Informed by sensations of weight, we open to the possibilities of a situation, orienting to the present moment.

How therapy clients experience their weight is basic to an understanding of their individual orienting processes. One of the most obvious examples is when the momentum and energy of the session build to creative integration. This is the novel experience often described as the moment of "aha!" These experiences of spontaneous adjusting create shifts in the energy, shape, rhythmic expression, direction, and flow of the client's movements. At such moments, a client frequently reports feeling "lighter" and more energized. Attuned to these shifts, the therapist can observe and the client sense how subtle changes in weight influence the whole of experience.

At the same time, a background experience of body weight lends us our unique, ongoing quality of being and behaving, our own particular style of orienting. Here the experience of body weight is expressed in a variety of postural types.[2] Each of us has a specific and habitual postural configuration that takes shape within the first three years of life. Every postural pattern is the adaptation of the individual to the physical (gravity, earth, space) as well as social aspects of the field. Through an awareness of their body-weight sensations, clients experience their postural styles.

In depression, a fixed postural formation emerges. The client often feels a heaviness pressing down upon her, and under the burden of this continued oppressive weight, standing or sitting upright requires so much effort that she appears to be on the edge of falling down, falling in, or falling over. Even breathing seems a chore. In order to fill her lungs, she must lift her collapsed ribs. So much work is required to simply inhale that the following exhale emerges as a depleted collapse. With such an exhausted burden to move around in these depressed forms, the patterns of posture, gesture, and gait appear as lethargic and leaden. The person's responses to either internal or environmental stimulations are slow, and characterized by sluggish energy.

Because proprioceptive awareness is dulled in the unaware act of "de-pressing" one's experience, the individual experiences her heaviness as an environmental intrusion, something pushing down on her from above. Preoccupied by her passivity, she cannot support the weight of her body. She collapses into the earth, "giving in" to the forces of gravity. She needs to move her heavy load, yet avoids the intense effort. She feels unable to stand on her own two feet and seeks something or someone to shore her up physically and emotionally; the nearest wall often serves as an effective leaning post. Or perhaps there is a person, either real or continually searched for, on whom she can lean.

A strikingly different example of fixed postural formation is found in certain forms of intense and chronic anxieties that convert easily into panic and crash suddenly into despair. Instead of giving in, this individual all too readily resists gravity's downward force by tensing his muscles, lifting himself up, and charging through space as if marching off to do battle. He constantly pulls himself upward to counter the forces of gravity. He can neither sense his weight upon the earth nor come to rest. With no resting transition, he is all too ready for his next anxiety-laden response. These responses might be to an event in the present or to a memory, idea, or some vague sensation of past experience.

Rather than appearing loose and at the edge of falling in, over or down, the chronically anxious individual makes himself rigid, as if to ensure that he will not break apart. The overall constriction of his body limits his breathing pattern. Movements emanate from his upper chest, while his abdomen remains overly compressed.[3] To inhale, he must pull up his already lifted rib cage and force air inward. This pattern dramatically reduces his intake of air and resembles the gasp reaction that happens in fright. His diminished breathing and chronic muscle tension gravely limit his proprioceptive awareness. The clear and necessary sensing of body weight becomes dulled.

Our experience of weight depends upon the interplay of background physical forces as they come to bear upon the three boney units of weight—head, rib cage, pelvis—which balance on the spinal column. The center of gravity (located just behind the naval and in front of the fifth lumbar vertebra) is the point where gravity *falls* through our bodies, allowing us to achieve harmony and equilibrium among these three units. It is from this center that fluid movements emanate. The manner by which each of us has come to align these three units of weight creates his or her unique postural configuration, and contributes to our diverse experiences of body weight.

In particular styles of depression, one can observe the client's head and rib cage collapsed and dropping downward into the pelvic bowl. The center of gravity is well below the navel, and the feeling reflected is burdened and deflated. In this collapsed position and with a concomitant lack of initiative, the depressed person feels pressured, crushed down into the earth. If, during the therapy experiment, the client shifts the center of gravity by lengthening her spine, separating her rib cage and pelvis, there is an immediate change in organizing processes and an accompanying shift in experience. Whatever excitation exists within the depressed pattern—anxiety, sadness, enthusiasm—emerges almost immediately.

With overbearing anxieties, the three boney units of weight stack in a different manner. The head and rib cage pull up and away, shifting the load of the upper body backwards; the pelvis is forced to rotate forward to balance the load. In this anxious configuration, the center of gravity is raised from just below the navel to the upper part of the torso. The individual is unable to feel the stable earth beneath his feet: he is "rest-less." As in the case of the depressed individual, when the head and rib cage are re-aligned on the vertical axis of the spine and in relation to the pelvis, the person senses more of his weight on the earth. Breathing patterns deepen immediately and are accompanied by an instantaneous feeling of relief. Emotions that have been avoided previously now surface.

These fixed postural descriptions are broad brush strokes of two orienting styles that are each inextricably linked to a distinct and individual experience of body weight. All our postural configurations include our accumulated proprioceptive experiences—all the unique ways an individual has adjusted within his or her surroundings throughout a lifetime—and serve as rich sources for psychotherapy investigation.

The Developing Experience of Weight

The ability to experience body weight is forged in early infancy through the emergence of developmental movement patterns. Our sensations of body weight in relation to gravity, earth, and space are made and discovered through movement. For example, resting on his father's shoulder, the two-week-old raises his wobbly head in search of novel stimulations. The action requires effort, as the heavy head is difficult for the newborn to manage. Doggedly repeating the act, the infant learns to distinguish the weight of his upward-moving head from the rest of his body, which subtly presses downward to counterbalance the movement. Emerging out of the infant's *internal* need and the enticing environmental stimulation, the pattern takes shape.

When the dyad is relatively well matched, the infant feels secure. Receiving as much assistance and support as is developmentally appropriate, he moves freely within his immediate world. Attention flows easily between his bodily sensations and environmental stimulations. From this generally stable background, a clarified body-weight experience forms.

When the match between infant and caregiver is chronically difficult, the dyadic relationship strains. Routinely stressed, the sensitive infant tenses, shuts down, and focuses away from sensations. Smoothly shuttling between an experience of body and other is inhibited. What was once the infant's appropriate, spontaneous resistance to an untenable circumstance becomes rigidified, a habitual way of being. Movement patterns grow inflexible, proprioception dulls, and the sensations of body-weight experience diminish.

The earliest relational experiences of deeply disturbed clients have been fraught with this kind of tension and strain. Often, traumatic circumstances within these clients first six months of development have produced deep constrictions in movement. The essential body-weight experience that accompanies the formation of pattern has been profoundly disrupted. For others, relational experiences in the first six months of life were stable enough to enable a relative facility of movement and sensations of body weight; even so, later traumatic disruptions in dyadic relations have inhibited not only the ongoing emergence of pattern, but also have distorted earlier patterns, diminishing the child's capacity for body-weight sensation.

In either scenario, the ability of these clients to orient themselves—to feel *here*, and in clear relationship to their own bodies and to their immediate environments—was grievously interrupted in either infancy or childhood and continues to be so. Now, as adults, that deep disturbance in sensing weight and the concomitant psychological issues create enormous difficulties. These clients are unable to manage or regulate their emotions and are caught in rigid and repetitious ways of connecting to themselves and the world: obsessive, compulsive, and addictive behaviors; ideas of grandeur; and/or feelings of paranoia.

How individuals experience their sensations of body weight determines how they experience themselves in relation to the other. It is a significant aspect of therapy, then, to reeducate clients' neuromuscular systems so that newly developing sensations of body weight organize and provide an experience of stability and security. With stable and secure ground, clients open to their own excitations, which sharpen and define. The clarified sensations of body weight enable clients' levels of excitement to match in intensity their levels of muscular activity. Now the energy of their emerging curiosity or interest is consistent with its expression. The continuity between themselves and their environments is enhanced through developing sensations of body weight.

To fully appreciate the role of weight in the processes of orientation for the adult client, we need to note further how sensations of weight emerge throughout early life. The following sections describe the background role of gravity, earth, and space in the emergence of two developmental movement patterns. The first pattern, yielding,[4] serves as the background for all later emerging anti-gravity patterns that move the infant up and away from the earth and through space. Inherent to all yielding are fundamental issues of finding and experiencing support.

The second pattern is the Moro Response, an early startle reaction that is present in the first three months of life. This whole-body reaction underlies the later development of more highly coordinated and individuated patterns of movement. The Moro Response allows the infant to adjust to a shift of body weight in relation to the sudden withdrawal of support. It is prototypic of the infant's ability to discover support once it has been lost. Disturbances in the fluid assimilation of the Moro Response and related issues of disequilibrium are background to the various maladjustments within the field.

The movement processes that engender change for the maturing infant throughout the developmental time line are functionally similar to those of the adult in the here and now. Using a somatic/developmental frame, the therapist can analyze the client's present moment behaviors. By observing and breaking down movement patterns into their most basic components, the therapist notes incomplete or unfinished patterns that create disruptions in the experience of body weight and disturb present functioning. Because these early developmental patterns exist as part of the adult's later and more complex movement processes, they can be stimulated into awareness in the adult. The client's presently dormant patterns activate and take on new mobility, compensatory patterns are simultaneously inhibited, and the coordination between support and contacting improves. With a thorough, first-hand knowledge of developmental patterns, the therapist can shape and refine experiments that will heighten and enhance the client's orienting capacity.

Yielding

It is through the experience of resistance, one force opposing another, that infants become aware of themselves orienting to the world. These resistances are, first and foremost, experienced through physical forces of gravity, earth, and space, and they influence the emergence of every developmental movement. The infant experiences the resisting force of his own body meeting the background forces intrinsic to the field whether in his responses to touch—for example, being stroked or patted—or to passive movements elicited by the caregiver—for example, being rocked, carried about—or simply in the active repetitions of movement patterns such as kicking or waving. The field is made known through our resisting it.

Experiences of resistance vary with shifts in muscular tensions. If the infant is moved abruptly, muscles brace to meet the changing forces of the field. If she is moved gently and slowly, there is no need for her to tense. In the latter experience, the infant's flow of tension is minimized and the resistance is less apparent, yet still a part of her experience. A change in muscular tension gives infants (and later adults) their sensations of weight and orients them within the world.

Just after birth, the infant placed belly down on her mother yields or releases the weight of her body to gravity. She draws toward the surface of the earth which is experienced much of the time through the body of the mother. The earth, in turn, *responds* to the opposing force by an upward thrust met by the body of the infant. This is experienced as a slight pressure into the parts of the infant's body that touch the earth. The reciprocal qualities of yield and resist, the experience of *one opposing and adjusting to an other*, are present in every experience of meeting.

As the infant lies on her belly, flexor muscles along the front of her torso are activated subtly. When she rests on her back, the extensor muscles are stimulated, and while lying on her side, those muscles along the sides of the torso are excited. In each case, belly, back, or side, it is this increase in postural tone[5] that subtly draws the infant downward, and is responsible for the experience of body weight. To the degree that the infant yields downward onto the resistant surface, he or she will experience the earth's reciprocal support. And how the infant experiences the support of the earth accompanies the continuing formation of yielding.

Although infants come into the world with an overall postural tone, it is through their responses to being held, carried, nursed, and rocked that their ongoing elaborations of postural tone and their experience of body weight are shaped and further developed. The caregiver with a clear sense of his body and a concomitant clarity in relating to the other offers an experience of security to the sensitive infant. The infant senses a firm support and releases her body weight. She yields into the caregiver's arms.

Because deeply anxious or depressed and lethargic caregivers do not solidly experience their own bodies, they create holding environments that are tenuous, transmitting sensations that are less than secure. Of course, this experience, too, reflects in the continuing formation of tone, and inhibits infants' ability to release their weight into another.

There is a strong correlation between the infant's internal organic rhythms organizing various levels of excitation, and the quality or style of the infant's yielding. Those infants whose excitements build quickly and with great intensity demonstrate a different style of yielding from infants whose excitations are slow to build and are less easily sustained. For example, the hypertonic child who is not able to fully release his weight into the earth, often meets the other with fixed resistance. And, the hypotonic infant, in appearing passive and collapsed, does not easily engage in a healthy and necessary resisting of the other. These internal rhythms, expressed through yielding, are again modulated or exaggerated by the caregiving environment. The slowed internal rhythms of an infant with low postural tone who relates within a lethargic and non-stimulating caregiving environment will produce a different yielding pattern from that of an infant with high tone, relating within an overstimulating environment.

As the infant moves from a horizontal support of the earth to the experience of vertical support, sitting or standing, an underlying experience of yielding remains. The quality of releasing into the earth influences the quality of all movements up and away from it. As the hypotonic child grows older, his inability to yield easily manifests in a lack of sufficient energy to complete his actions and he responds to stimulations with a slow and often uneven expression. Conversely, the hypertonic child's reactions are very quick and sometimes erratic. He is often unable to finish one activity before going to the next. Because the yielding experience sets a foundation for the child, it is crucial to his emerging dynamic development.

The Moro Response

As yielding is about experiencing the weight of the body in relation to the supporting earth, the Moro Response is the infant's reaction to loss of support and experiences of *falling* through space. Emerging at birth and continuing through the first three months of life, the Moro Response is elicited when there is a perceived but subtle shift of support of the head—back and downward in relation to the rest of the body. As the head suddenly lowers backward, the infant immediately experiences its weight. This happens when the head is not well-supported by the caregiver in lifting or moving. If the child is lowered, face upward, onto a supporting surface, the slightest change in the position of head to the torso will stimulate the Moro.

In the first phase of the Moro, the infant experiences an immediate loss of support. Because the undeveloped extensor muscles along the back of the spine cannot yet support the weight of the infant's heavy head, it drops backward, and the shoulder blades draw together. At the same time, the infant's arms extend, draw to her sides, and slightly behind her torso. Extending arms and fingers in this phase of the Moro is a global and diffuse response to the experience of falling.[6]

In the second phase of the reaction, the infant contracts the more capable flexor muscles along the front of his torso in an attempt to prevent the fall.[7] This activates another global response as the head flexes and both arms cross the body while the fingers grasp. The grasping assists the infant in discovering any object that will help regain balance. In the act of grasping, the object rushes to the foreground. The infant discovers stability and begins to learn the possibilities of finding support once it has been lost.

For the first few months after birth, the infant's primary pattern is that of flexion, which keeps each part of the body curled inward and close. When the sensitive Moro is elicited, it overpowers the infant's flexor pattern and brings her into extension. A new function is organized, that of expanding into the environment. It is a new relation. *Before infants feel the weight of their bodies falling through space, the act of extending into the world is not readily available to them.* The second half of the Moro returns her into the flexor pattern to recover from the falling episode.

In time, as the Moro Response naturally recedes, other patterns emerge to service newer functions. Replacing the Moro and arising out of it, are equilibrium reactions, more sophisticated falling responses that emerge in approximately the fifth month of life. Now when the infant falls forward or to the side, he extends both arms simultaneously. Touching the earth, the arms push down so as to support and protect the infant from meeting the surface with too much force.

When equilibrium reactions come into play, the infant gives up the initial anti-gravity grasp so necessary for balance in favor of extending his arms and hands for support. There is a vast psychological shift as the infant moves from grasping onto the other, whether caregiver or object, and clinging to support, or extending toward and pushing off the other, that is, finding and creating support. In the earlier grasping situation, the flow of movement is contained, constricted, and bound. Because the arms are flexed, attention is focused near the body. Extending, the infant directs his attention toward the environment, and the flow of movement is free and streams outward. His maturing ability to extend into the environment demonstrates a greater freedom in the world, while the grasping pattern of the younger infant reflects greater dependency on another for support.

Although falling is a momentary occurrence, it fills the whole field of experience. The infant learns something about overcoming dangers in the always challenging environment and about the adventure of losing everything. In those developmental patterns that move the infant up and away from the earth there is a quality of falling—leaving center, shifting weight, and reaching out. Thus the ability of infants as well as children and adults to move through the world depends upon their ability to continually lose and recover equilibrium. Orienting is supported and defined by the falling experience.

Caregivers whose *body-sense* is minimized are disturbed in their ability to respond spontaneously and adequately to a child. When such a caregiver experiences a diminished capacity to sense himself and the infant, he may move about or tend to the child in ways that are generally insensitive, clumsy, or coarse, not providing the required physical or emotional support necessary for the child to feel secure. In these situations, the infant must tense her muscles in an attempt to resist the subtle yet continuous threats to her equilibrium. Later in development, the child holds herself tight and sometimes appears immobilized. Ready to clutch or grasp onto someone/something, she apprehensively awaits the next assault and prepares to withstand whatever comes her way. This behavior assists the child, and is an attempt to make herself safe.[8]

For infants and children thriving within an environment that is both challenging and nurturing, healthy falling responses teach the potential to restore security and equilibrium. As they develop internal supports, these children begin to risk the losses involved in moving out and into unknown territory to discover the next solution to another developmental dilemma, which is often experienced as play. Assured of discovering and re-organizing their equilibrium, these children will be more likely to experiment. In this relatively secure situation, every new exploration becomes a statement of the child's faith in a world that is uncertain, yet manageable.

Orienting Possibilities and the Adult Therapy Client

The following section is devoted to brief case studies of two adult psychotherapy clients with very different styles of orienting. Sharon holds herself rigidly tight, as if to prevent any possibility of falling apart. Rhonda holds herself so loosely that she appears to be falling down. As Sharon is all too willing to act out her impulses, so Rhonda is all too willing to give up on hers.

As we view them, it will be clear that their movement patterns always express some meaning and convey a sense of who these adults are and how they live within their worlds. The somatic/developmental experiments I chose for each elicit and reveal the structures of their organizing processes.

For Sharon, sensations of yielding and the concomitant experience of support is the primary focus of our work together. For Rhonda, the heart of the experiment is discovering lost support. While disorganizing each client's present pattern of functioning, the experiments also provide a greater repertoire of movement possibilities for them, creating a different, more fluid orienting experience.

Sharon: The Process of Yielding and the Experience of Support

Sharon is a slight young woman who appears to crouch rather than to expose herself to whatever she imagines surrounds her. To create the crouching pose, she hunkers down by pulling her head back and in, folding her upper torso over her pelvis, and contracting her buttocks. In the process, she rounds her spine so entirely that her tailbone tucks between her legs. To complete the self-constructed bulwark that is her standing posture, she holds tight the muscles along the back of her thighs, creating the slight bending of her knees. She conveys the overall picture of someone about to spring up and out at any provocation.

Sharon keeps herself so compact that it is difficult for her to allow much of any interaction either in or out. This is replicated in her limited breathing pattern, a shallow and forced exhale and a weak and constricted inhale. While her abdominal area is squeezed together, pulled upward and toward her diaphragm, the muscles of her spinal column pull downward, creating pressure on her spinal cord.

Tension in both the organic and nervous systems and their muscular envelopes generate background stress for her, and any sensation emerges from an extreme constrained experience.

With her dense, hypertonic muscular tonus, Sharon cannot deeply experience her body resting. She feels cut off, ungrounded, and describes herself as "floating away," the polarity to her extreme muscular tension. Left with the disturbing sensation that she lives as if in a dream, she reports that she feels her actions are not her own. As she is disconnected from sensing and physically dissociated, she misinterprets her internal signals. She often translates her unclear body cues into terms both dramatic and vague; her movement expressions build to an equally dramatic "as if" emotion, an expression that seems out of sync with the original situation.

The gestural patterns that emerge from the tension of Sharon's muscles, organs, and nerves are erratic in nature. Her overall rhythm is a continual bursting and halting. Tension builds abruptly, immediately. The flow of movement is forced out with pained effort, and instantly retracted. The bursting and halting style is a major contributor to her frequent rages. Her raging impulse explodes outward and almost simultaneously is held in and back. Continued, this process leads to exhaustion and disintegration. With her general restlessness, and the rapid build up of her excitations, Sharon is often on edge and expresses feeling "out of control." She frequently argues with others; the repetitive altercations are for her forays at feeling that she is really present. Her unending stress is etched in her tense face: her forehead crumpled with worry, and a persistently lost, terrified expression in her eyes.

The Therapy

Sharon arrives highly agitated. She has just had a confrontation with "the guy in the deli." He misunderstood what she wanted and was rude to her. She wants to rage, and expresses a shred of awareness that this is her usual, habitual manner: as she argued with the man, she reports, she realized that she could not sense her body and felt "numb and disconnected." Feeling "less real," she became immediately terrified, and proceeded to become more angry and defiant.

"It must be absolutely terrifying not to feel really here. What is it you feel now?" I ask. Sharon replies as if she need not consider the question. "I feel nothing. That freaks me out. Will I get better? What can I do?" Her rage dissipates as her underlying and overwhelming anxiety surfaces. I answer her questions and offer my sense of confidence in her resources and our therapeutic process: "Yes, you will get better. It will take some time. Would you like to experiment?"

For the six months we have been working together, Sharon and I have been integrating somatic/developmental experiments into the therapy. A willing participant, she now finds the bodywork crucial, both during our sessions and in experimenting at home.

I ask Sharon to lie on her side on a padded mat in an almost fetal position. As it resembles her standing posture, it poses no threat.[9] I tuck a folded, thick cotton blanket under her head and roll up several more, shoring them in front of her torso, between her knees, along the back of her legs, and along her spine. Using several twelve-pound cotton sandbags, I rest one on top of her thigh, one touching the top of her head, and the last touching the soles of her feet. Now contained on all sides and at top and bottom, Sharon says she likes feeling "tucked in."

I ask her to feel the floor touching her side. As she gains some awareness of the floor beneath her, I ask her to pay attention to her abdomen. She replies, "I'm so tight. I always feel tight everywhere." I ask her if I can place my hand on her belly. She consents. Touching her, I sense my own body and begin to breathe more deeply and evenly. Inviting Sharon to breathe and to feel my hand on her belly, I note that her tension begins to soften. Surrendering, she says, "I like your hand there."

As we continue, I ask her where else she might like me to place my hands. For the next several minutes, she guides my support discovering that my touching her forehead, the back of her neck, and her abdomen feel best to her. She moves my hands from place to place and soon begins to release, feeling her body resting on the floor. Although this has been emerging through prior somatic/developmental experiments, the sensation is new for her. The experience is being etched into her nervous system, and it becomes more accessible as we work.

Sharon sighs deeply several times, and I notice weeping. Wanting to connect the clarity of her experience and its expression, I ask if she will say the words, "I feel sad." Sharon replies, "I feel sad. I don't remember my mother ever being with me like this." Her weeping deepens, and the area from her throat to her belly shakes in an even and gentle rhythm. Rather than fight her feelings, she gives in to her experience of vulnerability.

As her tears subside, I take Sharon's hand and place it on her abdomen, resting mine on top. At the same time, I match my breathing rhythm to hers, making my exhale audible. After a few moments, her exhale lengthens, and allows a more sufficient quantity of air to enter on her next inhalation. "Do you feel my hand on top of yours?" I ask. "Yes. Your hand is warm," she replies. "Can you feel your hand underneath mine, and resting on your belly?" "Yes." Moments pass, my hand on her abdomen, our breathing rhythms matching one to the other, and I ask if I can take my hand away. "But I want you to remember where it was," I add.

Sharon continues breathing more deeply and reports that she has a "sense-memory" of my hand over hers. I say: "Feeling your own hand resting on your belly, will you say to yourself, 'Right now, I'm here.'" Sharon is willing to repeat the phrase, first to herself, and then aloud. The more fully she experiences the meeting of her hand and her abdomen, the more clearly she knows she is "here."

Now she pushes her hands and arms into the floor to bring her body to a sitting position. As she levers herself off

92

the floor, her awareness of her body-weight sensations is deepened. I ask her to attend to her body. "The floor is very much with me," she reports. The greater constrictions of her seated posture now produce a more shallow breathing pattern.[10] This is as much change as she can support for the moment.

Seating myself in front of her, I ask her if she will look up at me, and wonder if she will be able to include me in her experience. To do so, Sharon must lift up her normally contracted head, a real risk for someone as guarded as she. To help support the newness of this action, I tell her to continue feeling her pelvic bones press onto the floor as she raises her head. She follows my instruction, and slowly her gaze meets mine. Immediately, she takes a deeper breath, as do I. Then I ask her to place her hand over her belly again, once more repeating the words, "I'm here," which further reinforces her power to support her own experience in the presence of another.

Psychodynamics

The work of therapy usually begins with encouraging the client to experience his or her anxiety. For someone as hypertonic and deeply imploded as Sharon, this is contraindicated. The consistently terrifying environment in which she was both abandoned and sexually abused had forced her to hold tight, an attempt to support herself. These muscles now form the fortress of her body. She barely senses herself and with a nervous system so easily overstimulated,

Sharon's powerlessness simply overwhelms her. Her defense is to rage to exhaustion and collapse.

Sharon's outrage is appropriate, but the neglectful and abusive figures of an earlier environment are now projected outward; she feels as if the other person is always out to get her. She lives the anxious victim to her own aggressive impulses, which, of course, boomerang with every angry outburst. She is left with exploding rage and then the sudden inhibition of its seemingly uncontrollable expression. This behavior is that of many abused children who, enraged with their abusers, instantly panic at the thought that their anger might kill the other, or that it might incite the other to kill them.

Existentially threatened during her early life, Sharon pulled inward and away from the external environment. She still lives with the persistent feeling and construct that releasing or surrendering herself to the other will be a danger. The yielding experiment was offered so that she could experience her body weight resting onto the earth, bringing inner and external environments into fluid relationship, and creating a fluid experience of self. I placed blankets and sandbags around her so that she could experience support along her periphery. The kinesthetic interaction between Sharon and the blankets and sandbags and my hands created an external pressure that encouraged the softening of Sharon's muscular boundary. Each part of the experiment was added incrementally so that she could gradually release her weight, feeling more and more whole—more and more *self.*

As the container, or the bones and muscles, are sensed, it is possible to experience the weight of the contents, or the organ system. Sensing her internal and organic rhythms, she was able to experience and contain her emotions. As the intensity of muscular and organic tensions changed and relaxed, she was sad, wept, and was able to articulate her experience. Now she is more capable of sensing her body, and managing the intensity and flow of her emotions.

As the session closed, I invited Sharon to place her own hand on her abdomen as a kinesthetic reminder that she can give herself the kind of support she has always longed for from others. The yielding experience and other such somatic/developmental experiments build a more stable and secure client/therapist relationship and provide a solid and dynamic background to the therapy.

Rhonda: Losing and Making Support

Rhonda is pear-shaped, neither tall nor short, with a softness to her muscles. Out of this softness exudes an attractive quality of kindness. She enters the room with a thumping gait. Her lower limbs feel so heavy to her that walking requires special effort. Routinely her hands clutch the edge of her sweater; the weight of her arms stretches it out of shape as she pulls it downward. The front of Rhonda's torso, her chest and abdomen, collapses inward, and her organs descend like a classic teardrop, as if falling into the pelvic bowl. Congruent with this motion, Rhonda presses her head almost imperceptibly forward and down.

Her musculature indicates Rhonda's hypotonic postural tonus. With such low tone, she does not have adequate muscular support, and must lock those areas that feel weak, in particular, her knees. When she locks her knees, her pelvis rotates forward, and this motion causes her low spine to arch pronouncedly. The rotated pelvis places the heads of her upper thighbones precariously in their sockets. From the weight of her displaced torso, pelvis, and legs, each of her feet collapses, rolling inward. All these grave imbalances pitch her body too far forward.

Light in quality, Rhonda's gestures often lack sufficient energy to complete her actions. When she is angry, for example, she forms a loose fist and strikes at the chair's arm, but the energy of the movement never completes itself. Her hand hovers just above the chair and leaves air between it and her fist as if to cushion the blow. An incongruous half-smile highlights the action.

Rhonda's gestural pattern is restricted to making movements close to her body. She rarely reaches her arms outward and into a full extension; her gestures are primarily from elbow to hand, while her upper arms appear glued to her sides as passive nonparticipants in the experience. Even while discussing matters of grave concern, she constricts her upper arms. The pattern demonstrates the discontinuity between her needs and their expression.

Rhonda rarely takes a full, deep inhalation. Every so often, the lack of ample air propels her to gasp, which forces air into her lungs. The gasp is followed by a sudden gushing exhalation, after which she begins to hold her breath again.

While the sudden collapse of the exhale leaves her feeling empty and deflated, her extended holding on exhalation creates a high degree of tension. She reports feeling tight in her abdomen and chest.

This same lack of energy resounds in her speaking patterns. Rather than reaching me, her words seem to fall out of her mouth and onto her lap. Her unsupported verbal articulation is directly related to her lack of breath support. The stream of her exhale expires in mid-sentence, and Rhonda runs out of air before she has finished her part of the dialogue.

In such a general state of collapse, Rhonda does not have a clearly articulated experience of body weight. Her body alienated, she feels her weight as some kind of external force bearing down upon her. Living is frustrating much of the time, just too much to contend with. Unable to cope, Rhonda acquiesces to gravity. It is as if there is always something in her way, and she cannot push it aside in order to get on with her life. The dilemma is constant. Her ever-present frustration and concomitant exhaustion leave her detached. Her emotions are weak and enervated, and she is unable to state them in depth and with clarity.

The Therapy

Rhonda sinks into the big green chair, slumps to one side, and props her head onto her arm. Her eyes are cast downward and she is silent for some moments. I feel the beginnings of some tightness in my chest, and imagine the silence to be her unspoken demand for rescue. I take a deeper breath. Slowly, Rhonda reveals that she cannot do anything different. She wants to lose weight, she says, but she can't. She'd like to find a better job, but she doesn't have the strength. She's been thinking about taking an art class, but she doesn't do that either. After every comment, she sighs and descends further into the cushions of the chair.

I ask her if she will attend to her sensations in the moment. She reports feeling ". . . heavy and tired all over," her usual experience; it is this continual heaviness and exhaustion that diminish her approach to the various challenges of her day. I silently test two interventions in my mind. In one, we work *with* her resistance. I ask her to exaggerate sinking further into the chair. We have done this type of experiment before. It leads to further deadening. I imagine it and feel dulled. In the second possibility, I imagine going *under* her resistance, doing something completely different. Instead of her usual *falling in*, I imagine creating an experiment that will have Rhonda *fall out*.

I invite her to get out of her chair and try an experiment that involves a prop, the "Buddy Band." The prop is a long, thick industrial rubber band that is two inches wide, and approximately twelve feet in diameter, and covered with brightly colored soft cloth. It is commonly used in therapy with distressed or developmentally delayed children.

At the spot where several padded yoga mats have been laid out, I ask Rhonda to stand behind me and hold the band around my lower abdomen and hip sockets. I tell her to hold it tight enough so that she can easily support my weight as I drop forward onto the mats, my feet remaining in place, but with enough slack so that I can fall without crashing. Because of the fear sometimes associated with falling, I demonstrate the experiment several times myself so that Rhonda understands the movement before she attempts it.

Rhonda is appropriately intrigued, but wary. She agrees to try. I hold the band securely around her hip bones and she drops forward. Her arms and hands never completely extend to support her fall; instead, she responds very slowly to the rapidly approaching ground and then crumples at her elbows and knees, her landing cushioned by the mats.

She and I now spend some time working through her irritation with me and the "dumb" experiment. A feeling of shame soon rushes to the surface, and Rhonda's eyes begin to tear. When the tearing subsides, we discuss what happened. Both of us had observed her inability to respond quickly to the demands of gravity. I tell her I had noticed that as she fell forward, she had been looking directly downward at the floor. Her upper arms had been held closely to her body and their inhibition had prevented a completed outward extension. I suggest that on her next attempt, she try looking up and out. Shifting the focus of her eyes will encourage an accompanying outward reach of her arms and hands, I say.

Rhonda experiments again. This time she practices lifting her head up and outward. It is now easier for her to support her fall with her hands and arms. With every attempt, Rhonda exercises new-found faculties, and is able to more and more aggressively support the weight of her body. When she has finished experimenting, I invite her to attend to herself while standing. After several moments, she reports that she feels "taller and lighter." Further, we discover that her torso, pelvis, and spine have a new sensation of lightness. Her arms feel "weighted, and tingle." Her legs feel "solid under me," and her feet feel "planted." I notice that her breathing pattern has shifted, and I tell her so. Rhonda monitors her breathing and says, "My chest feels more open, and I'm able to take in more air. That was fun."

Psychodynamics

Rhonda's habitual style of orienting emerges from a background that is experienced as ambiguous, and gives the impression that she is disinterested in both herself and her surroundings. In this experiment, she called upon all her resources to perform. As she had only herself to rely on, she needed to focus her attention acutely.

In her first attempt, when she crumpled to the floor, she became irritated, blaming the experiment (rather than me) for having exposed her incompetence. She became the familiar victim to her own experience. Beneath her irritation lurked the beginnings of a familiar and omnipresent shame. Folded posture, cautious gait, controlled gestures—all kept her predictably contained and minimized her imagined potential for failure and the requisite, accompanying shame.

In our earlier sessions, the shaming experience would have been attended by a chorus of self-recrimination and comparisons to some idealized other: "I should have done better. Only a fool would be so clumsy." This time, Rhonda's shame moved her to tears and then swiftly passed. Beyond it, she was able to become sufficiently interested in experimenting again. When her body weight shifted from upright to all fours, she sharply reorganized her experience. She was forced to become present. Resolute and determined, she continued. The appropriate amount of aggressive energy necessary to complete the movement was discovered and harnessed. Learning to support her fall, Rhonda experienced an essential satisfaction in her newfound ability.

The falling process activated an earlier and currently inhibited developmental pattern. Rhonda was able to locate her inhibitions to fluid functioning: her routinized, downward gaze; her inability to fully extend her arms outward; and her slowed reactions, all aspects of her depression. Her usual lumbering and oppressed orienting changed with the rapid shift of weight. She became more capable of adjusting to the ongoing and previously unacknowledged background of gravity, earth, and space, phenomena that had formerly been alien to her.

The falling experiment became the springboard for our continuing dialogues in therapy. In the process, the background structure that accompanied her collapsed style was gradually revealed and experienced: the grievous loss of feeble earlier support; overwhelming disappointments; and the overbearing inner critics who haunted her.

* * *

Both Sharon and Rhonda lacked a coherent experience of themselves in relation to their immediate environment. They were out of touch and isolated. This breach in the whole of experience is the result of disturbing events that had left each profoundly distrustful. They feared not being supported, and therefore, being unmet. The somatic/developmental experiments we used created change in each client's habitual relation to gravity, earth, and space, encouraging each to discover her inhibited and unacknowledged resources. The psycho-physical function that is inherent in the original patterns was stimulated: releasing into the earth to allow and mobilize support; falling and extending into the world to discover and create support. Experiments in pattern restored the original underlying, yet incomplete supports for contacting. What emerged was a more flexible orienting experience.

For such clients who have lived deeply routine, fixed styles, a change in orienting, even a momentary one, is appreciated. These enormously novel experiences are remembered, referred to, and further enhanced in the anticipated therapy.

Chapter Three Notes
Primary Orienting Experience: Gravity, Earth, and Space

1. M. Todd, *The Thinking Body* (New York: Paul B. Hoeber, Inc., 1937).

2. Posture also refers to the multiplicity of positions we assume in order to make continual moment-to-moment adjustments.

3. In a natural breathing pattern, movement begins at the level of the lower ribs and moves upward toward the collarbones and simultaneously downward toward the pubic bone, creating a wavelike motion in the cavities of both abdomen and rib cage.

4. This pattern was so named by Bonnie Bainbridge Cohen, founder of the School for Body/Mind Centering, and is part of the larger more expansive system she has created. She now refers to this pattern as "yield and push."

5. Postural tone is the overall level of muscle tension while one is at rest, and reflects the ability of the muscle to respond to both the *inner* and *outer* environment. First developing in the womb, postural tone is a complex biological process of both genetic and environmental factors that influences and is influenced by early motor experiences, and is categorized as high, low, or moderate. These degrees refer to the level of the intensity of tone, as well as the balance between the tone of the flexor muscles (the front of the torso) and extensors (the back of the torso).

6. According to Kephart (1968), the body of the infant is undifferentiated at this time of development and its parts function globally rather than separately.

7. During the first months of infancy, the flexors are more developed than the extensors and are more prepared for use.

8. With certain children, the hypertonicity may be less obvious, as the intensity of muscular tension may be held so much closer to the bone, or often in the connective tissue and organs, while the muscles closest to the skin become weak and flaccid from the imbalance. In these kinds of children, the startle may elicit an immediate freezing that may be held for some time, after which the child begins to cry inconsolably and eventually collapses, limp and disoriented (Fraiberg, 1982). Although very different in style to the immobilization or hypertonic response, the appearance of hypotonicity or collapse—an indication of resignation—is just as much a resistance to the perceived and overwhelming forces of the field.

9. Placing clients in positions that are so contrary to their routinized posture often elicits extreme anxiety and must be advanced only in graduated steps.

10. It is easier to release habitual, postural constraints in a horizontal position than in the vertical, as the individual does not have to contend with the forces of gravity.

Chapter Four

Reaching and Being Reached

Through the rhythms of life, human experience concerns itself with meeting and being met, influencing and being influenced, reaching and being reached. In the joining of one and another, the individual becomes part of some larger experience *flowing into and with* the greater field. From the *I*, a *we* appears. Separating from the larger, sensing difference once more, the reach completes itself. From the *we*, an *I* emerges. Reaching, we realize our selves.

Reaching is a whole body event. The sensorimotor organs of mouth, eyes, ears, and limbs measure the distance between one and the other. How far away is what I long for? How near is what has become terrifying? Sometimes the distance feels vast as if meeting is simply impossible. At other times, the distance shrinks, offering possibilities to feel part of another. Subjective, relational, and perceived, the experienced distance gently expands, abruptly contracts, lightly envelops, or harshly represses.

For both therapist and client, the observation and experience of reaching patterns are a vital method for exploring the relational field. In the building of relationship, clients extend toward their therapist, carefully measuring the distance between themselves and the other. In the act of reaching, clients discover to what extent, at any given moment, they wish to include the other in their experience.

Therapists also measure the distance between the client and themselves and adjust their creative efforts accordingly. They are sensitive to the varied ways their clients reach toward them in the hopes of establishing closeness. They also observe when their clients anxiously pull away, fearing that to be close to another is somehow to lose oneself.

Within the course of the psychotherapy session, all movements carry meaning for both therapist and client. And the meaning always arises from the context in which the movement occurs, the client/therapist field. A keen awareness of reaching functions on the part of therapist and client attunes both to the ongoing relationship that builds during the session. The therapist draws the client's attention to his or her gestural pattern, and both become privy to important and necessary psychodynamic information that organizes and emerges within the relational dyad.

When the therapist invites the client to recreate, exaggerate, or attempt the opposite pattern, awareness heightens. The client has little time to calculate his maneuvers and thus maintain a vigilant control over his behaviors. The emerging and spontaneous material can be a surprise to the client who has kept it so repressed that it is a secret even to himself.

In health, when the object of interest is perceived as safe, inviting, and within reach, the movement pattern emerges as uninhibited and smooth. Movements are distinct and directed toward the other. The person opens her body, increases her receptivity, and extends toward the other with certainty. In the process of reaching, she feels her eyes, mouth, arms, hands as being *mine*—an integral part of herself. As she senses her body, whatever she grasps becomes part of experience. Including the other encourages her belonging in the world.

When the object of interest is perceived as unwanted and uninviting, the healthy person pulls away with similar conviction and clarity. She is unwilling to become part of the other. Spontaneously she closes her body and exposes much less of herself. Her receptivity diminished, she declares that the "other" does not belong to her experience. It is excluded.

In dysfunction, however, the person neither reaches toward the other completely nor pulls away with confidence. The reach becomes routinely "stuck in the middle," and the pattern inhibits, disrupts, and demonstrates a position of constant, unresolved compromise. The body loses flexibility and is not fully sensed. For the person who yearns for closeness and is terrified by it, the other often appears frightening, perhaps too close for comfort. From this conflicted experience, an ambivalent gestural pattern emerges: for example, the arms may stretch in the direction of the other yet clutch firmly to the sides of the body; the fingers curl inward at their tips; the upper torso and neck constrict and pull back; and the head faces down and forces the eyes to peer upward. On the other hand, when closeness is experienced as persistently beyond one's grasp, a markedly different gestural pattern may occur: for example, the mouth may open wide; the arms stretch outward, locking at the elbows; the fingers extend with such emphasis that they appear to bend backward; the head and upper torso press forward; and the eyes gaze fixedly, without connection to the other.

In these examples, such interruptions in primary systems of support reflect the unique styles by which each individual has adjusted to his or her prior environment. Although these fixed patterns were once temporary and creative adjustments within a difficult, earlier field, they have since become repetitive and, therefore, disturbing to healthy experiencing.

This chapter focuses on the formation of reaching patterns in the infant and child as mediated by mouth, eyes, and limbs and the relationship of these early structures to adult experience. Just as reach patterns indicate the capacity for spontaneous adjustments within the primary dyad, they also exhibit the capacity for similar spontaneity within the client/therapist relationship. When therapists recognize how reach patterns emerge and become part of an infant's movement repertoire, they have a broad-based background from which to observe and understand their adult clients.

Once a comprehensive, phenomenological diagnosis is made, somatic and developmental experiments can be implemented to heighten awareness of missing sensorimotor supports. More and more of the client's resources are brought to relatedness.

The Developing Dynamics of Reaching

Infants rely on a developing language of body that enables them to reach out and experience the other, and in so doing, to experience themselves. Every infant's reaching pattern evolves as a pathway toward solving developmental problems or tasks. In the process of discovering the solution, the reach is made.

Reaching patterns, like other developmental movement patterns, emerge as a product of: the infant's internal dynamics (metabolic processes, anatomical constructions); the fundamental constraints of the physical field (gravity, earth, and space); and the unfolding relations within the social environment, which further organize his needs and interests (primary caregivers). The developmental pattern that emerges within this confluence of considerations is at first unstable and easily disrupted. Because the pattern has not yet been fully assimilated into the developing organism, there is a great deal of variability in its shape and form. This variability is the substance of creative adjusting.

It takes much practice for the infant's reach to become reliable and fluid—to locate in space what it is the infant desires, to discover the appropriate effort and the most efficient pathway toward the object of desire, and finally, to incorporate the other into the infant's experience with a final grasping onto. Each emerging pattern carves its path through space, relying on the coordination of one part of the body with the other and in relation to the environment. Through a series of reaching experiments, an increasingly efficient and better coordinated pattern forms, and more of the environment can be integrated into the self.

Infants whose interactions with their primary caregivers are satisfactory often enough throughout development acquire a balanced rhythm of reaching and being reached. The infant's needs are experienced by the caregiver and met, modulated, or exaggerated in ways that serve healthy contacting. In spontaneous and creative adjusting, the infant's reaching pattern reveals a harmonic quality, as the effort used in shaping the movement comes into balance with the intrinsic energy of the need.

With some infant/caregiving dyads, the infant is neither met nor encouraged sufficiently. In this situation, the reaching patterns that emerge are incomplete. These inhibited patterns alter the existing need by either exacerbating or diminishing it. For example, a ten-month-old infant in need of attention reaches out to pat his caregiver's face. The caregiver, distracted and lethargic, hardly notices the pat and does not respond. The infant, whose internal energy happens to build quickly and does not easily dissipate, soon becomes frustrated. His level of energy continues to elevate. A mounting excitement adds to the urgency of the moment and comes to bear on the effort underlying his gesture. The pat becomes a hit. Having been hit successively (and successfully), the caregiver *now* notices the infant and attends to him.

If the caregiver is generally distracted and vague in her responses, this infant will frequently resort to a forceful and frustrated style of finding attention. The reaching pattern that evolves for him is sharp, constricted, and intense, and one that reinforces, and even exaggerates, the accompanying excitation. A dyadic, relational rhythm develops as the infant's reaching pattern conforms to the emerging constraints of the field. The movement patterns of the caregiver are also affected by this exchange, and the caregiver's rhythms and quality of pattern shift and adjust with the ongoing dialogue. For instance, with the right amount of prodding from her child, the caregiver's distracted and lethargic style may suddenly burst into sharp, intense explosions, after which she collapses and constricts.

Another infant with a similarly distracted caregiver may form a reaching pattern that is wholly different. When this infant needs attention, she too reaches out to the lethargic caregiver and is met with vague disinterest. This child's excitations, in contrast to the first infant, are slow to build and dissipate easily. Rather than an agitated display of concern, this infant signals to the caregiver in a halfhearted manner and soon gives up on her own interests. She collapses, withdraws, and curls her arms and legs inward. While the first infant's reach pattern exaggerated the excitement of his need, this child's languid and flaccid reach serves to diminish the intensity of her excitement. With a repetition of these kinds of infant/caregiver dialogues, this infant's style of reaching becomes flaccid and inhibited.

In both scenarios, the enormous variety of potential reaching combinations for each infant has been constrained, limited, and directed by the possibilities within the respective infant/caregiver fields. The sequence of kinesthetic interactions within the relational dyad forms the ground from which affective exchanges emerge. These primary, kinesthetic interactions are the foundation for the child's, the adolescent's, and the adult's preferred patterns of relating. They set the affective tone that bonds one to another.

Let us focus in greater detail on the formation of one specific reaching pattern: how infants function when they are receptive to ongoing dialogues within the field, and when receptivity is blocked and fluid communicating obstructed.

The Rooting Response: Reaching with the Mouth

One of the earliest developmental patterns to emerge in the infant is the rooting response, or reaching with the mouth. Guided by her nose, the infant reaches with her mouth in search of the nipple. Once it is found, she grasps onto it and begins sucking in rhythmic bursts. In the grasping action, the infant takes firm hold of the other for leverage and support.

Latched onto the nipple, the infant's jaw and skull bones move in a coordinated fashion to enable sucking. When the head is well supported, the sucking action begins at the jaw joints. The upper jaw/skull bone moves away from the lower and backward. With this back and downward motion, the base of the skull levers into the infant's first cervical vertebra and creates a compressive force. The action reverberates down the entire spine. Next, the upper jaw/skull retraces its pathway and moves forward and up. The motion closes the mouth, lengthens the upper spine, and completes the action. The entire sequence creates a rocking of upper jaw/skull on the lower jaw. The neck muscles shorten and lengthen alternately. Reaching/sucking actions activate muscles along the back of the body via the spinal column as well as muscles down the front via the esophagus. In this way, reaching and sucking is a whole-body event.

In healthy, fluid functioning, the infant is able to adapt relatively smoothly to the task of nursing. She experiences the caregiver's support, reaches for the nipple, grasps onto it, and includes the other in her experience. When she is sated, she releases the nipple and separates; then she draws her attention inward and distinguishes herself from the other. Within this background of belonging, an experience of individuality emerges.

In situations of chronically disturbed functioning, the reaching, grasping, sucking action does not complete itself. Imagine a distracted, detached caregiver who does not carefully support the infant under his head and buttocks. The infant struggles to stabilize. He grips the muscles of his neck and abdomen. Reaching/sucking is impeded. The upper jawbone/skull is now held in a subtle back-and-down position, and the infant's mouth remains open. He is unable to grasp the nipple effectively. Tension mounts at the base of the neck and abdomen and generates strain in the muscles and soft tissues of the spinal column and the digestive tube. Motor coordination is impaired. Sensing is diminished. With repetition of these events, the infant becomes uncertain that comfort and nourishment will be forthcoming. Under these conditions, opportunities for a satisfactory affective connection between infant and caregiver are gravely restricted. The infant is left open-mouthed and with an ongoing frustration, dissatisfaction, and longing. He must struggle for what he most wants. He braces himself, helpless in the face of an unaware, neglect-ful, and unreliable other.

Now imagine a further example of the reaching impediment in the infant for whom sucking is automatic. This extreme disturbance might be the product of difficulties experienced in the womb, such as the presence of drugs, alcohol, the mother's extreme mental distress, and/or a cold and indifferent post-natal caregiving environment. To avoid the poverty of her intolerable existence, the sensitive infant abruptly withdraws her energy from the periphery and shuts down. Breathing patterns constrict, and tension gathers in the organ systems and the neural core. When breathing is severely restricted, sucking becomes automatic and the mouth is no longer a fluid organ of exploration. The infant does not sense the other as belonging to her, as an integral part of her experience. A deep and abiding breach of trust forms within the infant/caregiving field—an immeasurable and lasting wound.

Each developmental reaching pattern integrates into the nervous system, influencing as well as reflecting the whole of experience. Developmental patterns of mouth, tongue, and jaw, from which reaching and sucking eventuate, evolve and serve as a background support for the child's, the adolescent's, and the adult's behaviors.

The Adult Therapy Client

In disturbances of contacting, the client's eyes may stare or appear vacant, lips press furtively together or part involuntarily, hands clutch apprehensively or fold solemnly; or fingers point aimlessly or grasp in desperation. The instinctual need underlying the chronic and inhibited gesture has been left dissatisfied. The more specific the phenomenological diagnosis, the more precise the prescribed somatic/developmental experiment can be.

During the experiment, the psychological structures, or incomplete past experiences, move to the foreground. The elements that have comprised and shaped the pattern, that being: the client's history, biomechanics, and neuromuscular, emotional, perceptual, and cognitive features are no longer secured one to another. During the kind of transitions evoked in therapy experiments, greater variability in movement and an accompanying shift in environmental possibilities emerge. The client, anxious and excited, experiences the edge of new behavior. What was once fixed, unaware, and unavailable for use, now moves forward, offering spontaneity, creativity, and choice. Analogous to infant processes, the adult client's more fluid, adaptive pattern will need practice to become accessible and reliable.

In the following case vignettes, both therapist and client experiment with subtle eye, mouth, and limb movements. The experiments bring each client's existential concern to the surface. Embedded in Bob's every reach are questions of his very being: *If you don't welcome me, am I really here?* Cynthia, not wanting to appear as if she cares, reaches and immediately withdraws: *If you don't want me, I don't want you!* Brenda desperately grasps, attempting to secure the other: *If I cannot hold onto you, I've failed.*

Bob: A Description

Bob sits squarely in his hard backed chair. He is of average height and slightly overweight. His soft, imploring eyes reach toward me while the rest of him remains motionless. He holds his breath as if he is waiting for me to do or say something. The distance between us fills with expectation, and I feel suspended.

I note that Bob's skull presses back and down while his lower jaw remains slack, his mouth gaping. Seeming to defy and oppose the downward thrust of his skull, he shoves his shoulder bones upward. The force between his head and shoulders creates an intense pressure at the base of his neck and tenses the muscles of his upper back. A similar pressure at his low spine generates a severe pelvic arch and pushes his soft belly outward. The constrictions at both ends of his spinal column stress his nervous system.

Bob locks his upper arms and elbows close to his torso, as if he is trying to keep warm. His hands routinely gesture in front of his body and otherwise near it; rarely does he fully extend his arms to either side, opening and exposing his heart. Although his tight arm muscles bind his movements, his hands and fingers are unusually flaccid and appear to swim through the air as he motions. When he is excited, Bob separates his index finger from the others and extends it, as if to argue a point. But his movements are indirect and sometimes flail, and his point is generally not well taken. The bound tension of his arms and the contrasting looseness of his wrists and fingers reveal his difficulty in sensing these parts of his body. Lacking a kind of ownership ["This is *my* arm . . . *my* hand"], he cannot fully sense what he reaches for or grasps onto as part of his experience, as belonging to him.

Severely dulled in his sensations and constricted in his movements, Bob has only limited ability to contain and express his excitements. His enthusiasm abruptly either converts to a kind of manic exuberance or explodes in chaos. Or Bob immobilizes himself and seems to avoid feeling at all.

The Therapy: In a Psychotherapy Training Seminar

Bob reports that he is angry, and that he does not feel well treated at his job. He is, in fact, "enraged" and so angry he could "kill *them*" because they are "killing me." He says that his killer feelings are directed toward other people he believes either have "wronged" him or are turned toward himself. I ask Bob if he would attend to his body while repeating the words, "I'm angry." Doing so, he lifts the toe-balls of both feet off the floor, one at a time, while the heels remain. The movement creates a rhythmic pattern—one-two, one-two, lift-drop, lift-drop—but it does not release fully into the floor, so each foot is left partially contracted at the ankles.

I ask Bob to change the movement's rhythms from a lift-drop to a lift-stomp, with the emphasis on the stomp, and to complete the act saying, "I'm angry." He experiments with both movement and phrase for about five seconds, then abruptly stops. His eyes well with tears and become even more imploring. A habitual and familiar experience emerges for him, desperate loneliness mingled with an abiding fear. I sense this to be a static experience, a well-traveled road. Closely identified with an earlier image of himself as an unwanted infant or child—his mother was cold, deeply depressed, and had more than a dozen children—Bob has formed a rejected and forlorn self as the perennial background to his relationships.

I comment: "First, you were angry. When you were asked to exaggerate that feeling, you swiftly killed it by filling yourself with desperate sadness. From what I know of you, you are raging and wanting to kill someone, beating up on yourself, or falling into a well of grief." Bob agrees: "I don't know anything else."

I take this as my cue and ask him if he will return to the experiment. "Let's build support for your angry feelings from the bottom up. Go back to your feet and gently push them onto the floor. When you sense they are under you, repeat the phrase, *I'm angry*." For the next several minutes Bob slowly feels his feet on the floor. Spontaneously, he begins to stomp, and I add the phrase, "'I'm so angry I could . . .' fill in the blank, Bob." "I'm so angry I could smash cars," he says. His embodied, emboldened anger is experienced and expressed for brief moments until helpless grief and then an incongruous smile or joke interrupts. This recurs with every interruption, and I invite Bob to find his feet under him until he senses his body and the energy of an angry expression.

His anger finished for now, Bob withdraws into himself. I wait with him, sensing my own breathing, and then ask, "What are you feeling now?" "Surprised!" he says. I tell him that when an infant or a child is surprised, he expands his chest, opens his arms, eyes, and mouth and gasps with the anticipation and delight of being met. Once met, the infant sighs with satisfaction. I demonstrate the response, eliciting a smile from him, and he soon joins me. He extends his arms, opens his mouth, and inhales deeply. Air is forced into his lungs, and his tight upper ribs expand.

A full and deep exhale follows. We do this together several times. His eyes never leave mine. "You mean I'm welcome . . . really?" He laughs.

I turn his words around, "Try the sentence, 'I am really welcome here.'" For the next ten minutes we work with Bob's capacity to breathe in and out deeply while stating "I am really welcome here" to me and the other group members. With practice, Bob's excitement becomes easier for him to sustain. I up the ante and ask him to continue the experiment while he stands and faces the group. Upright, Bob exposes more of his body to the others and becomes more receptive. He also experiences his feet directly beneath him, which supplies a much needed support for his retracted pelvis.

Bob reiterates the phrase, "I am really welcome here." He jokes, gets tired, repeatedly forgets the sentence, remembers, and persists. Now and again he reminds himself, "I need to feel my feet." With each practice, his expression grows more authentic. The gestures that emerge solidify his experience and embody it further. Now he spontaneously points to himself when he says *"I,"* and opens his hands and extends his fingers toward the others when he says, ". . . am really welcome *here.*" Once the experiment finishes, he reports that he feels more relaxed in his neck and shoulders. I notice that his eyes appear to rest in their sockets. His breathing is deeper and more even, and it moves into his upper chest. His neck is lengthened. His gaping mouth is closed.

"You are now finding supports for enlivened experience." I tell him, "As the foundation is made solid, your persistent feeling that people are 'killing you' and the reciprocal need to defend yourself by 'killing them' will dissipate. Good riddance to that." Bob laughs. The session ends.

Psychodynamics

Bob's habitual and seriously insufficient style of breathing sharply curtails his expectations and satisfactions. Unable to expand with desire, he anticipates the frustration and despair of not being met. He chronically holds his breath on the inhalation. This pattern creates a bound muscular tension throughout his body—the kind that erupts in unsupported, falling-apart anxiety and the expression of its avoidance, rage.

Bob inadvertently cuts himself off from the nourishment of deep breathing and constantly re-stimulates his earlier pattern of longing. The object of desire is far off and cannot be found. His eyes beseech the other for attention, approval, love. They express unspoken feelings of deprivation and the accompanying violent helplessness of not having what he wants. Intermittently, his eyes flicker with terror. The threat of asking for, and maybe *getting* what he wants can be as great for him as the crushing disappointment of *not* getting. What if he reaches out and is not met? What if he *is* met, and then loses what he has just received? He is stuck in a fiercely ambivalent, compromised position. In desperation, he reaches toward, and simultaneously holds back in dread. This conflicted pattern reflects in bodily discrepancies and splits: head pressing forward, upper spine and pelvis pulling back, arms held tight and close to his torso, hands flaccid/flailing, legs held rigid, and feet askew.

As a child living with ongoing neglect, Bob learned to inhibit his breathing and tighten his body. To hold back from a desolate, indifferent caregiving environment is creatively adaptive and temporarily supportive. Why reach out if there is no one reaching back? Giving up seems preferable to feeling despondency and harsh disappointment. But the chronicity of the pattern continues to suppress Bob's excitements as an adult, and to discourage their energetic expressions. He is filled with the pain of his own inauthenticity. He is also filled with resentment.

I encouraged Bob to press his feet onto the floor and spontaneously stomp in order to discover support for his angry expression. Doing so allowed him to move away from the muddle of an early and rigidified wound, and from the ensuing character of a victimized child. The experiment helped him to identify with his adult self. He felt entitled to his anger and to its vital, genuine expression.

The novelty of his experience surprised Bob. I demonstrated for him an infant's or child's expression of surprised delight: a full inhale; open eyes, mouth, and arms; and an extended spine. This was followed by a deep and satisfying exhale. He mirrored the pattern. The incremental, fluid shifts in his breathing and gesture cultivated a pleasurable expectation for him. Bob completed the act, and in doing so his earlier script of never having been met, for that moment, was rewritten.

Cynthia: A Description

Her well-formed muscles lend Cynthia the appearance of sturdiness, and she appears to be capable of handling whatever comes her way. Her shoulders elevate, her rib cage lifts and expands outward, her arms hug resolutely to her sides, and her elbows pull backward. The overall pattern makes her seem taller or bigger than she is and adds to the initial impression of confidence that she gives.

The weight of Cynthia's body rests on the backs of her heels. To prevent herself from falling backward, the muscles along her thighs and legs constrict, and her knees lock. Her muscular tension is exacerbated by the backward and downward press of her head, which creates strain in the base of her neck, jaw, and upper spine. The natural curve of her low back exaggerates and tips her pelvis forward.

Cynthia holds tight, determined to keep herself under control. It is as if she is persistently pulling up, back, and away from some impending catastrophe. The rigidity of her postural pattern limits her full range of movement possibilities, the extent of her excitements and their expressions. Ungrounded and with so much energy held in her upper body, Cynthia experiences intense pressure generating in her head. She is besieged by an almost continual flood of unwanted thoughts.

As she pulls herself up and away from the possibility of environmental dangers, she also pushes away feelings of hurt, sadness, and disappointment, the *internal* dangers. When she feels threatened, she secures her arms still closer to her torso. Only anger seems permissible for her, and Cynthia often uses her customary belligerence to intimidate. Her pugnacious attitude serves to keep others out, but it leaves her with unbearable loneliness and with deep feelings of exclusion. Nevertheless, she bolsters herself and remains continuously alert. This behavior keeps her away from not only what she is frightened of, but also what she hopes for.

The Therapy: Clinical Encounter

Cynthia says she feels a constant "struggle" with her mother. "She's always hovering over me . . . telling me what I should be doing. She even tells me what to eat! Our relationship has never changed. She never gives me what I want."

"What is it that you want from her?" I ask. "I want her to leave me alone," she quickly replies. With further investigation, Cynthia clarifies her statement, saying that she wants her mother to acknowledge and respect her. "What would respect feel like?" I ask. She contemplates my question and her eyes fill with tears. "I think I want her to love me," she says with a look and sound of incredulity, as if wanting a mother's love were a novel notion.

I ask Cynthia to stand up and imagine her mother. How she organizes her experience is clearly revealed by her standing posture. Visualizing her mother, she says, "She's holding back from me," but when I probe further she cannot describe how she knows this. "It's just something I feel," she says. I ask Cynthia to notice her body. As she turns her attention inward, she senses intense tension developing at the back of her neck and shoulders. She has sought treatment for these chronic neck/shoulder pains through massage and chiropractic and has found only temporary relief. I ask her to exaggerate the tension in these areas. In order to recreate and magnify the pattern, she notices that she must tense her neck and pull back her head, an action that jams the base of her skull into her spinal column. Simultaneously, she lifts her shoulders up and slightly backward. She also notices that her arms hug to the sides of her torso, her elbows are pulled backward, and her fingers are tensely grasped. I ask her to exaggerate this posture and again to visualize her mother. Immediately she exclaims, "I'm holding back too! I never realized that. I feel sad for both of us." She sighs.

The Following Week

Excited, Cynthia talks about her "profound" experience of the prior session. "I'm always so tense. Mostly around my mother, but even when I'm not with her, I do the same thing. I'm not sure why, but I'm anxious a lot," she confides. We continue to experiment with her habitual and braced postural pattern. She tenses and pulls back her neck, lifts and tightens her shoulders, pulls her elbows backward, and simultaneously hugs her arms to her sides. Her fingers grasp. She looks like a boxer waiting for an opening. Cynthia holds this position for some time, feeling the inherent struggle in the pose.

Silently, I entertain two possible interventions. In one, Cynthia curls her hands into fists, pulls back her arms even further and finishes the restrained action with several jabbing movements. I feel uncomfortable as I imagine this experiment. It is too early in our relationship for Cynthia to safely reveal her anger so completely. Not enough supports are in place. Instead, I invite her to unwind her tensed, grasped fingers, and then to follow the natural, sequential, unfurling action of the pattern until she is fully extended. This will unravel her compromised position, I surmise.

At my request, Cynthia relaxes her hands and slowly and deliberately reaches out. The movement initiates a dynamic and energetic release through her arms, shoulders, chest, and head. At the end of the movement's sequence, her stance is more relaxed and both her arms are fully extended. Only her head and eyes are cast downward, interrupting the flow of action. "Will you look directly at me?" I ask. She lifts her head and eyes to meet mine. Then she startles, suddenly retreats, and pulls back and in. She notices this immediately. "I just got scared and pulled away from you," she says with surprise. "I'm afraid to reach out. I'm not sure why."

Cynthia explores her anxiety further in a series of experiments as she extends her arms. I realize there is little movement in her back. The physical blockage results, in large part, from lifting her rib cage up and pulling it back. A lack of flexibility just behind her heart indicates insufficient support for her reach.

Now we experiment with Cynthia lying face down over a large oval-shaped, eighty-five cm. ball. As she yields into the ball, she audibly exhales. The ball lends support to her ribs and pelvis. I further support her upper spine by gently tapping the area between her shoulder blades. She breathes deeply. Between tapping motions, I rest my hand lightly on her back. Once I sense that she is more relaxed and open in her spine, I ask her to stand and extend both arms directly overhead. Then I kneel in front of her, placing my hands on her feet. The downward pressure of my hands enlivens the underlying supports—her feet—for her upward reach.

When Cynthia fully attends to the reach of her hands and the press of her feet, I change my position. Standing behind her, I place my left hand on her right shoulder blade and press lightly downward and toward her ribs. At the same time, I gently grasp her right arm with my right hand and slowly pull it up, creating a subtle sensation of traction. Her shoulder blade slides down, inhibiting tension, her arm stretches up, facilitating a greater range of motion. I recreate this hands-on technique with her other shoulder/arm.

After my adjustments, Cynthia rests her arms by her sides. "My back and shoulders feel so much looser and my arms are heavy. And I still feel my feet," she says. I ask her to continue feeling her feet and to reach toward me. She experiences, and I observe, the backward pull of her upper spine as she reaches out. Cynthia's conflict is clearly visible as she exaggerates her position. "I want to reach out to you, but I'm not sure what you want. I mean if you want me to." I ask her to repeat the sentence, but with a slight variation. "I want you, but I don't know if you want me." At hearing these words, Cynthia cries, then sobs. When her tears pass, she says, "My neck feels so much better. I can't remember the last time I felt pain-free. I feel good."

Psychodynamics

In the smooth and uninhibited standing and reaching pattern, our feet must subtly press onto the floor to give the movement its underlying support. The reaching capacity of the upper extremities is influenced by the underlying *pushing support* of the lower. Reaching moves from the fingers, through the lower and upper arm bones into the shoulders, rib cage, and spine. The sequence is an energetic flow from periphery to center that then circles back out from the center to the periphery. At the end of a fully committed reach, the fingers grasp onto the object—the longed for assistance and support.

Earlier reaching patterns of past experience have fixed, one onto another, shaping and forming the present character of Cynthia's postural configuration. Such fixations of postural pattern are an amalgam of arrested developmental movements, distorted, yet protecting against the incomplete and avoided aggressive expression of the full pattern. Embedded within these arrested patterns, the structure of unfinished experiences and their accompanying affect endure.

As she imagined her mother, Cynthia felt Mom hold back from her. When I asked her to draw inward and sense her body, Cynthia became enlightened: it was *she* who held back! To heighten awareness of her pattern, I invited her to exaggerate her stance. Cynthia became aware of how she positions herself in relation to her mother. Her initial dilemma of *what she [Mom] does to me* was now experienced as *what I do to myself.*

To be accepted by the significant and primary figures of her early life, Cynthia had to hold down her excitements by pulling back, in and away from another, a creative adaptation. Holding down, holding back, and holding in express a compromise of conflicts: *I neither reach out to you with all of myself, nor do I completely hold back.* The persistent struggle expresses itself in the present moment of the session and in the presence of the therapist. The appropriate background anxiety of an unclaimed and repressed excitement surfaces. Anxiety, if unsupported, leads to feelings of exclusion and isolation. Once Cynthia's sadness emerged, her anxiety dissipated. She was present.

At our next meeting, Cynthia and I turned our attention to her postural pattern, a composite of psychological functions. Cynthia exaggerated her retracted pattern and, in the process, released excess tension. Her release, coupled with the reaching of her arms, hands, and eyes created a more vulnerable stance. Cynthia startled; she was afraid to reach toward me and did not know why. She tightened around her spine, abruptly withdrew her arms, and flexed her fingers. Her reach was interrupted.

I used a large oval ball to construct a support for Cynthia's lower ribs and pelvis. As she lay over it, I began tapping her upper spine to enhance sensations and thereby facilitate movement. Between taps, I rested my hand on her upper spine. Both actions helped to reduce her hypertonicity and created flexibility in the smaller muscles of her spinal column.

As Cynthia stood and reached her arms overhead, I used my own hands both to inhibit the chronic spasticity surrounding her shoulder/upper spine (pressing the shoulder blade in and down) and facilitate the improvement of muscle tone (pulling the arm away from the shoulder). The traction created much needed space around her arm/shoulder joint. She developed additional support for her standing posture: a looser spine, relaxed shoulders and arms, and the sensation of her feet on the earth. Cynthia felt relieved. Now that she was more related to her body and the immediate surroundings, the psychological material that had been unfelt and unavailable could emerge. When Cynthia reached toward me again, she recognized the ambivalence of her uncoordinated movement pattern: her arms reach forward—yes!— but her upper spine tenses and pulls back—no! Each force locks in a battle to dominate the other. Then the psychological function set within the inhibited, ambivalent reach is discovered, "I want you, but I don't know if you want me." The pattern disorganizes, as previously fused components of sensing, feeling, perceiving, and thinking loosen. In transition, Cynthia teetered at the edge of new behaviors. Sobbing, she then committed fully to her present experience.

When the psychophysical structure of the pattern revealed itself and was experienced and expressed, Cynthia's routinely strained neck freed. Today, tension in Cynthia's neck, a symptom of her inhibited reach and the accompanying repressed emotional expression, continues to be an important signal for her both in and out of the session.

Brenda: In a Psychotherapy Training Seminar

The following experiment took place during a week-long training seminar attended by psychotherapists. It serves as a poignant example of a mismatched dyad. Participants were paired together. Person A was invited to lie supine on the floor while person B sat at his partner's head. Partner B held a soft cloth toy in front of A and slowly moved it from one side to the other. Partner A was invited to track the ball with eyes and head.

What follows describes the experience of one experimenting dyad.

Brenda lay on the floor, her arms extended at a forty-five-degree angle from her body and her legs separated about twelve inches apart. Her head was placed on a cotton blanket that was folded several times to create support and lengthen her habitually constricted neck.

Henry, her partner, appeared both eager and anxious. An unfelt muscular tension informed all his actions. His gestures burst forth abrupt and sharp, only to be almost simultaneously held back. In contrast, Brenda's gestures were so languid that at times they bordered on collapse. Her eyes, glaring and exposing their whites, maintained a high degree of intensity, as if all energy were localized there.

As the experiment began, Henry waved a small cloth doll in front of Brenda, keeping it about sixteen inches away from her face and moving it erratically from side to side. As soon as Brenda settled her eyes upon the doll, Henry jerked it away. To keep it in view, she had to keep up with Henry's tensional rhythmic pattern. She was moving her eyes and her head to a beat that was clearly not comfortable for her.

After a few moments, Brenda shut her eyes. When she reopened them, Henry swiftly yanked the doll from side to side, and up and down. She strained to follow his movements, but her valiant effort was short-lived. Again she closed her eyes and then sank onto the floor. Her hands opened in a subtle gesture of abdication. The position of resignation reverberated in her breathing pattern, which was significantly reduced and held on her exhalation. Henry, genuinely enjoying his experiment, did not seem to notice that his partner had dropped out.

As Brenda had grown listless and withdrawn, I asked Henry if I might try a different intervention. With Brenda's permission, I took a soft brush and stimulated the palms of her hands. She watched attentively, "I like that feeling," she said. Then I took a small hard rubber ball and dropped it into her palm, repeating the movement in a steady, even rhythm. "The predictability [of the movement] feels soothing to me," she offered.

I took another ball and repeated the steady, rhythmic tempo in Brenda's other palm. Slowly, her hands began to grasp the balls. To exaggerate the emerging grasp pattern, I held each of her hands with mine, pressed her fingers firmly around each ball, and pressed the balls into her palms. I took several deeper breaths, and so did she.

Now Brenda slowly rolled to her side, sat up, and eagerly told the group of her "significant experience." At the beginning of the experiment and as Henry had waved the doll from one place to another, "I had to work hard to keep up," she said. The dyadic experiment reminded her of earlier, familial experiences, when she was asked to do more than she was capable of doing. At such times Brenda said, she pushed herself in an effort to meet her parents' (in particular, her father's) expectations. "I was always such an overachiever. I had to get approval for doing well, and I had to do well or I was a failure. That's still true," she added.

As the experiment with Henry proceeded, Brenda had become frustrated at the "unpredictability" of the doll's placement. "I really wanted to gaze at it and have it come to me. I wanted it to be easy. I didn't want to work so hard. And then I just gave up. I felt myself going numb." Brenda recognized the familiar pattern, the desperate attempts to overachieve, to be "more than I really am," ending in resignation and despair.

Abruptly, Brenda stopped her story, "Do I look different?" she wondered.

"What feels different?" I say.

"My eyes," she answered, "I can't say exactly how." "Yes," I agree, "Your eyes are softer and they appear receded in their sockets. How do *I* look to *you*?"

Taking her time, Brenda answers, "I don't feel my eyes pushing, and it's easier to look at you. I'm not working so hard." Slowly looking at the other group members Brenda says, "I feel more comfortable with all of you."

Psychodynamics

The difficulty within the Brenda/Henry dyad emerged immediately as Henry kept the toy much farther away than was comfortable for Brenda and seemingly beyond her reach. Likewise, his gestural rhythm appeared out of sync with hers. Involved in his own enjoyment, Henry noticed neither Brenda's discomfort nor her efforts to shut him out. The mismatch of the dyad brought her routinely inhibited visual pattern into sharp awareness.

Seeing is a balance between our reaching toward the object and allowing the object to come toward us. It is a combination of resist and yield, an aspect of all contacting episodes. Brenda's eyes, pushed forward in their sockets, appeared rigid and stuck. In this style of reaching, a fixed stare, much of the peripheral vision is restricted, and this drains supports from both organism and environment.

Under these strained conditions, the object of such intense focus looms so large that bodily experience diminishes. Dyadic tension between one and the other does not easily equilibrate. Meeting is fraught with pressure.

The interruption in contacting was clearly visible—Brenda's anxious and piercing wish to reach out and grasp onto the much desired, but elusive object. Working with direct touch, I stroked Brenda's palms with the brush to stimulate sensation. To build supports incrementally, I rhythmically dropped balls into one of her palms and then the other. The weight of the balls gave her the sense of holding onto something. Soothed, she gradually clasped her fingers around the balls, gently receiving them into her hands, a natural conclusion to a grasping experience. I wrapped my fingers around Brenda's, and pressed the balls deeper into the cups of her hands. Her awareness heightened.

When she was seated, her experience in one sense modality, touching, transferred to another, seeing. Brenda released the perpetual searching pattern of her eyes. Looking around, she felt "easier" and "more comfortable" with both the therapist and the group—an experience of inclusion.

* * *

In the preceding scenarios, the shape of each person's reaching pattern expressed his or her individual style of approaching and withdrawing in sequences that were fluid or restrained. In each case, I observed that the person needed to reach out for assistance and connection but was too anxious to do so. In reaching toward what he or she most longed for was the fear of not being met and the attending discomfort, disappointment, disillusionment, and shame. The ambivalence was displayed in the person's whole body. The prescribed somatic/developmental experiments addressed subtle reaching disruptions and engaged the core of each person's existential/psychological conflict.

Chapter Five

🔉

The Upright Stance

The imperative to right ourselves, to remain vertical against all disturbing influences, is fundamental and with us from our very beginnings. No matter how infants are positioned, they attempt to right themselves—nose vertical, eyes and mouth horizontal. And when they are placed on their bellies, their eyes invariably find the horizon as their heads orient in the upright position. So begins a sequence of movements that brings the child to standing.

Standing upright is the inevitable consequence of healthy human development. It is something we move toward, grapple with, and ultimately discover. Unlike other species, we are kept waiting to attain our upright stance. Once we have arrived, our head sits atop a vertical spine. Our eyes are well-situated to reach the extending horizon. There is far more to discern: the field expands, and with it the excitement of who we can become. Our anxiety arises, for there is now so much more to lose.

With bellies exposed, we face each other head on and so confront ourselves. We state our intentions and sense our vulnerabilities. Upright, we experience the risks inherent to adjusting within this larger, more complicated field. Again and again we lose our balance, fall, and even fail. The demand to assert and maintain ourselves erect continues throughout our lifetimes.

To learn to support ourselves in the face of conflicting forces is central to psychotherapy. The style or manner by which we seek to right ourselves is most evident in our stance. In a sense, the upright stance is the client's history as it manifests itself in the present. It is the creative integration of all his or her earlier patterns of experience, and the result of present efforts to differentiate within the field.

In the process of psychotherapy, it is crucial for the therapist to attend to clients' upright expressions—their stances as well as the subtle head/spine adjustments that emerge throughout the session. How people have held onto their sense of right, their authenticity, while confronting the other is immediately revealed through their upright positions. Although this information can be observed and worked with in the seated posture, for me it is significant to have clients get out of their chairs. Poised and standing, people are more open, receptive, and available. As they stand, I observe and they experience the system of underlying sensorimotor patterns that either support or undermine their upright realities, along with concomitant experiences of authenticity.

When we are upright and well-supported, our head and feet align relative to a vertical axis. The balanced relationship between our head and feet allows us to know our position in relation to the surface of the earth. Sensing, perceiving, and feeling are enhanced. Transitions from one movement to the next are flexible and smooth. Harmony exists in the mover and the move.

When upright postures are habitually misaligned, we cannot find easy equilibrium. The head does not rest lightly atop the spine, nor move freely side to side and up and down. When the head is so placed, it is impossible for us to clearly sense the weight of the body resting into the feet. Imbalances between the head and the neck influence the muscular tonus of the entire body and form rigidified, habitual attitudes. Although a fixed attitude and stance hampers graceful movements and fluid contacting, it is nevertheless an attempt to stabilize in the world. For those whose stances have become disrupted in this way, the pattern feels familiar, but the person lacks a sense of authenticity. He is estranged from his surroundings. The extent to which the person's upright position is fixed is the extent to which adjustment is being blocked.

When observing upright experiences, therapists are not interested in deviations from a vertical "ideal." Rather, they follow any subtle movement and note whether the client's habitual stance has shifted and becomes either more pronounced or uninhibited. For example, the shortened and contracted spine of the client may suddenly lengthen or a head that has been formerly upright now abruptly tilts to one side. Such departures contribute crucial clues to the client's internal states and relational experiences. As therapist and client explore these elusive yet obvious expressions, new material emerges.

As in all emerging patterns, stance forms from a background of prior experiential sequences. No behavioral pattern completely disengages from an earlier field, so former psycho-physiologic functions are contained within the present of an upright structure. The antecedent background exists as part of the present, influencing and being influenced by it. Resistances to contacting present themselves as inhibitions in upright pattern. These can be seen and readily understood from a developmental perspective. The therapist views the emerging pattern as branches of a larger sequence, and the roots of psychological disturbance make themselves known. In this way, the field of awareness expands.

This chapter elucidates the developing progression of the upright stance in the infant and its relationship to adult psychological functioning. It explores several movement patterns that build the background supports for adult upright experience. The chapter concludes with the case vignettes of two clients, each of whom has difficulty experiencing her sense of right, as is evident from the expression of her upright stance.

The Anatomy of Upright Being

The structure and function of every detail in the human body are designed to support a vertical stance. To balance upright requires a harmony of all parts of the organism in relation to each other *and* to the environment. When each of these parts organizes near the spine, the supporting center, we can easily explore our surroundings. Movement in any direction is graceful, fluid, nearly effortless. Energy is freed and made available for creative adjustment. The experienced situation is direct, immediate, and sensed with excitement.

The spine serves as a column that supports the boney weights of the head, the rib cage, and the pelvis. The column curves in such a way that these weights either rest (head), hang (rib cage), or brace onto (pelvis) the spine. Unified by the line of gravity, each boney weight is centered directly over or under the other. Weight transfers down through the spine, shunts downward/forward at the sacral joints to the center of each hip socket (located on either side of the pubic bone), and continues through the thigh, the center of the knee, the leg, and the ankle joint. The entire leg is fashioned so that each foot falls precisely under the hip socket and perpendicular to the ground. It is the spine that supports the limbs when we are upright. This phenomenon is uniquely human.

Twenty-six bones of the foot and many more joints, muscles, tendons, and ligaments enable us to adjust freely and spontaneously to the complementary forces of gravity and earth. Touching and in touch with the earth, the foot permits us to push into the ground and to pull it back. We propel ourselves through space. In upright standing, our fundamental support is located at the level of the lower spine, pelvis, and legs. This allows for greater differentiation of the upper limbs. The fine coordination that flows between shoulders, arms, hands, and fingers is basic to our orienting and manipulating within the field. When we are on two legs and feet, gravity's center is at the level of the navel. This placement allows for maximum flexibility and variability in movement pattern.

Difficulties of Being Upright

The delicate arrangement of boney weights carefully balanced along the spinal column allows flexible muscles to use a minimum of effort when resisting the forces of gravity. As it is not always easy to maintain equilibrium, stability is continually lost and found.

When equilibrium is *habitually* lost and the individual is unable to find steady ground, joints become strained, and muscles become stiff and limited in range. Parts do not organize near the center, nor do they balance in adequate relation, one to another. The relationship of spine and limbs is askew. Movements are inhibited. Standing upright and on two legs becomes stressful. The head no longer balances simply on the spinal column, and the feet no longer directly touch the earth.

As the stability and flexibility of the upright stance falter, vitality is given over to rigidity and immobilization. The body is blotted out, relegated to a province that is not part of experience. Readiness to respond is diminished. Lost is the sensuality of creative adjusting, and with it an inherent sense of rightness. The spontaneous rhythms of separating from and merging with another become erratic—contacting disrupts and fixes.

Such fractures in upright experience parallel a variety of splits in the self. Some people appear to be inflicting their will on gravity, bowing rigidly backward as they pull up and away from the earth. They appear removed, austere, unapproachable, and seem to have an air of superiority. Maintaining their ground, they hold fast and steel themselves erect. Over determined in their stance, they remain immovable and imposing. With any subtle shift in surrounding circumstances, they dig their heels even deeper into the earth. They report feeling the pain of hyper-muscularity. Closed off from the potential resources of another, they create a wall. Isolated, they imagine themselves sufficient, and self-righteousness replaces the lost sense of right.

The opposite of this rigidity is visible in cases of immobilization. These people bow forward and position themselves as supplicant. Unable to feel the ground solidly underfoot, they slump, shuffle their feet and shift their weight from side to side. They habitually surrender their own preferences. As they fuse with another, they are unable to separate fluidly, and thus, they sustain their dependency and abdicate a sense of right. It is always someone else who knows what is best. When their demand for sameness is threatened, their longing turns to rejection. What was once desired is now hated. In an expression that is parallel to the style of rigidity, they isolate themselves.

In either of these broad brush stroke styles, rigid or immobilized, the person is unable to appreciate or even tolerate the differences between himself or herself and others. Difference feels disturbed and separate, and leads to isolation, or it blurs and entices one to a frozen confluence. Habitually either resisting or constantly bending their wills, these people have grown impaired in their ability to respond spontaneously and to relate within the field.

Through an observation of upright expressions, therapists understand how clients position themselves in relation to the other. Captured within an upright form are patterns of intention: how this person has moved toward what is appealing, and away from what is not. As with a constraint in reaching functions, the client is often found stuck somewhere in the middle, moving neither fully toward nor fully away from the other. The incompleteness of movement pattern suggests the unfinished intention, the interrupted experience.

Upright Behaviors in Infant Development

Every pattern that emerges throughout development stimulates a set of neuromuscular relationships and forms dynamic connections between one part of the infant's body and the other, and to the environment. Each of the following developmental events demonstrates the basic energetic connections that are made within these patterns and their relationship to upright experience. Although modified through time, each developmental pattern retains it's essence and continues to serve a similar function in the adult's experience.

Righting and Pushing

Righting reactions begin at birth and integrate within the infant's developing neuromuscular system to maintain the head and body upright and against gravity in all positions and during movement. They are primary responses within the relational field. Righting reactions fall into two categories: reactions that orient the head vertically in space and perpendicular to the earth's surface; and reactions that align the head to the torso, enabling the infant to be well positioned for locomotion.[1] As they emerge, whole-body patterns of flexion and extension, previously formed in the womb, are slowly reorganized. In the process, infants learn to move smaller segments of their bodies independently and to engage in more coordinated activities. With every repetition, the muscular tone throughout the entire body is activated.

Righting reactions generally assimilate into the neuromuscular system to become other patterns, however, several remain active throughout human development. For example, when an adult loses balance and starts to fall, the head will right itself immediately to maintain a vertical relationship to the horizon. These reactions interact with the newly forming pushing patterns to organize all transitions from one movement to the next. The combination of righting and pushing allow infants to lift their heads, turn to the side, roll, position themselves on hands and knees, sit, crawl, and eventually stand. Righting reactions and pushing patterns facilitate the infant's processes of differentiation. They are also particularly important in designing treatment for the adult client.

Moving Up and Away from the Earth

To understand the interaction between righting and pushing, it is necessary to know the basic characteristics of all movement processes. Any movement that we make involves a shifting of weight which causes our bodies to push downward onto a supporting surface. In the act of pushing, the compression of the body's tissues against this surface stimulates our proprioceptive awareness, and we begin to sense ourselves as separate from the other—our bodies from the surface underneath us. While a shift of weight provides the stimulus for the emergence of righting reactions, righting reactions also initiate and support further movements. This will become evident in the series of overlapping developmental movements presented below.

An eight-week-old infant rests on her belly. Her curiosity and the enticements of a fascinating world stimulate her. She rights her head. To counterbalance the upward movement, simultaneously her body presses downward onto the supporting surface and weight shifts onto her shoulders. In the act of righting her head, extensor muscles on the back of her neck activate. The movement begins at the head and moves fluidly through the center of each vertebra and down the spinal column to complete itself. Through these subtle righting and pushing movements, the infant begins to differentiate her head, the periphery, from the spine, the center.

At three-months-old, lying belly down, the curious infant raises her head, and actively pushes her forearms onto the earth to see the world. The more she is able to lift her head and extend her spine, the more she can place the weight of her upper body on her forearms. The extensor activation enables flexor muscles along the front of the body to be systematically elongated. Elongation must take place before independent flexor control is possible. Again, the pattern originates from the head and arms and moves downward to the end of the spine and the lower limbs, which offer stability. A differentiation emerges between limbs and spine, and upper and lower body halves.

As development progresses, the five-month-old is able to better maintain the elevated position of her head, while pushing herself somewhat farther away from the earth. She can now drop her chin and glance downward, which stimulates more independent control of the flexor muscles along the front of the neck. The newly forming flexor tone balances the developing extensor tone. The infant either bears her body weight on both forearms symmetrically or shifts her weight from side to side by pushing from one hand to the other. These movements provide important proprioceptive information from the infant's shoulder girdle and upper extremities.

When the five-month-old rests on her back and presses her heel(s) onto the earth, her pelvis lifts. The weight shifts to the head, shoulders, and upper trunk as the body forms a bridge. The lumbar spine and the lower limbs coordinate, and the infant further discerns her upper body-half from the lower. And, when her back rests against the supporting surface, she is able to lift one leg at a time. This action activates the flexor and extensor muscles of the leg. At the same time, the flexor muscles of the spine deepen in tone, while the spinal extensors elongate.

At this time in development, the infant on her back can already rotate her head to one side, which is soon followed by the movement of her torso. The spontaneous alignment of her torso to her head brings the infant into a "side lying" position. This early rotational movement is the product of an underlying righting reaction in combination with the infant's increasing efforts to explore her environment. With the further differentiation of her body parts, the infant at five months actively rotates her head, pushes one foot onto the earth for leverage, and reaches with the same side arm, causing her to roll from her back to her belly. The integration of righting, pushing, and reaching patterns is a prerequisite for rolling—the organization of rotational movements around an axis. It is the first pattern of locomotion.

By the sixth month, the infant, on her belly, has more stable control of her head; she can extend it backward, flex it forward, and flex it to either side. These more refined movements further develop the tone of the extensor and flexor muscles of the neck, bringing them into balance. This is essential to an ongoing equilibrium in the upright position. The infant can fully extend both her arms, which shifts the weight of her upper body to the heels of her hands. Now movements of her head are better supported by the trunk and the limbs. She can also support her weight on one arm while making tentative reaches with the other. Propping herself on both arms and pushing downward, the infant pulls her knees up under her body. This movement activates the muscles of her upper chest and abdomen. Then the infant pushes from one hand to the other, slowly working herself into a quadruped position. Against this background of balanced extensor and flexor tone, the infant is able to distinguish more clearly between the front of her body and the back.

Throughout development, the manner by which the infant rights her head on her spine, influences the effort and shape of the downward pushing and subsequent reaching movements of both the upper and the lower limbs. And, the pushing and reaching movements of the upper and lower limbs, in turn, influence the righting of the infant's head on her spine. This is common to all developing movements as the prior patterns to emerge provide the ground from which the later patterns take root, and the later emerging patterns exhibit their ongoing influence on the underlying and preceding patterns.

All patterns of moving up and away from the earth enable the infant to differentiate the head from the spine, the head and spine from the limbs, the front of the body from the back, the upper body half from the lower, and all in relation to the environment. In standing, this ability to differentiate will translate into a reciprocal relationship whereby the lower limbs support the spine and the spine supports the upper limbs in their exploration of the environment.

How Disruptions Develop

As mentioned in previous chapters, continuous mismatches between the infant and the caregiver either at particular points in the developmental progression or throughout it affect the emergence of sensorimotor supports. In general, whenever there are chronic disruptions within the relational field, the infant learns to tense at the center of his body. In these kinds of situations, movements become inhibited; they do not clearly emanate from the periphery, the arms, the legs, and the head, and fluidly circulate toward the center of the body, the spinal column. As development progresses and the holding pattern continues, the young child's capacity to differentiate each of his body parts in relation to the others and to the environment is impaired.

When the developmental and relational sequence produces neither flexibility nor stability, the child's upright standing posture demonstrates the difficulties. For example, imagine that the child's neck does not sufficiently support the head as it moves in all directions. The resulting misalignment of his head and neck creates tension in the jaw, the tongue, and the throat. In response, the extensor muscles of the spine strain and the shoulders can elevate, especially during movement, causing the infant's arms to jam in their sockets and to constrain his gestures. In addition, the tight spinal extensors can exaggerate the natural arch of the low spine, and the pelvis rotates forward. Overpowered by extensor tone, the flexors weaken, and the child's belly protrudes. With the misalignment of his pelvis, the child's lower limbs are not well placed in their respective hip sockets and the ability to discover easy equilibrium is weakened.

In all, the alignment of the child's head and his feet relative to a vertical axis, so necessary to clarity in sensing, perceiving, and feeling, grows distorted. Every emerging pattern becomes restricted, and along with it, the child's style of connecting with himself and within his world. The manifestation of such types of misalignments, of course, varies with each child within his or her particular relational environment; there are as many outcomes as there are individuals.

As the child's development continues, chronic difficulties in the capacity to right the head on the spine and to push the limbs onto the earth produce a complex of psycho-physical compensations. These compensations can be observed in the overall muscular tone of the child's body. When the developing relationship between the extensor muscles and the flexor muscles is not well balanced, the child's ongoing transitions from one experience to the next are not easy. Adjustments lack fluidity and spontaneity. Just as habitually interrupted explorations inhibit the fluidity of a child's upright stance, inhibitions in stance act to further frustrate exploring. The euphoria of upright, independent excursions may be replaced with a fear of solitude and possible abandonment. The child experiences confusion between the desire to satisfy his own needs and the desire to rely on the other for satisfaction.

Dilemmas in Righting: The Adult Client

We have seen that interruptions in adult movements express previous and unfinished experiences within an earlier relational field. They affect the adult client's here and now through the presence of diminished authenticity: restrained sensuality, dampened curiosity, unresolved emotions, inappropriately inviolable loyalties, and fixed postural stance. All the movement patterns that arise throughout the therapy session reveal behaviors that either promote the client's sense of right or undermine it.

The case studies below explore the upright styles of two clients, Lisa and Karen. Both have great difficulty experiencing themselves while facing another. The chronic inability for each to achieve and maintain a vertical alignment profoundly influences her behavior, and her behavior influences her stance. While several distortions in support functions prevail, a particular pattern emerges in each session described here that sharpens the issue of the moment.

Lisa

Lisa is tall and long-limbed. Her head presses forward and is subtly angled to the right side, as if it is about to roll off her long, thin neck. Her shoulders pull back to compensate for the forward thrust of her head. In response, chronically misaligned muscles along the sides of her throat have become taut. When she is anxious and unsure, the forward angle of her head increases, her throat muscles tense even more, the skin of her neck reddens, and she averts her eyes. This behavior occurs when Lisa feels that someone is about to criticize her or gives her any hint of withdrawing.

Only the subtle movements of her abdomen reveal Lisa's breathing. The area along her shoulders, collarbones, and upper ribs is fixed and tight, and her inhalations and exhalations are not visible here. The top of her breastbone is depressed, and the superficial muscles along her ribs appear underdeveloped. The collapse rounds her upper spine and tenses and weakens the muscles along her back. This unsubstantial spinal support cannot easily maintain the action of her arms, and they appear, at times, ineffective and without the necessary power to express her feelings. Her dispirited movements demonstrate her lack of conviction, and she easily loses herself to another.

Lisa's pelvis is tight and it tips forward, which creates an arch in her low spine. Although her weight is some-what less than average, the pelvic rotation makes her belly protrude. The imbalances caused by her misaligned pelvis make it impossible for her to feel fully supported by her legs. In an attempt to counteract her lack of stability, she locks her knees. This gives her a semblance of solidity, but it creates an inflexibility and rigidity in the ankle, knee, and hip joints. Reporting that she never actually feels the steady support of her legs, Lisa complains of weakness in both her knees and her ankles. She is uncomfortable standing on her own, and often pushes her hip to one side, maintaining most of her weight on one leg and appearing to be uprooted.

The frailty in both her upper and her lower extremities leaves Lisa drained of energy. She lacks the readiness to respond to whatever comes her way. New situations feel awkward to her, and her solutions to dilemmas are indirect and clumsy. This style of relating is observed in her gait: she ambles forward and stumbles. She overcomes her chronic exhaustion not with a healthy aggression that lends itself to ongoing interactions, but with an iron will. She must be "productive," she says. While her solid determination has made Lisa a leader in industry, her presentation lacks conviction and reflects inner emptiness.

The Therapy: A Clinical Encounter

When the following session took place, Lisa had been coming to weekly therapy for approximately five years.

Lisa says she eats chocolate bars late at night. It is a repetitive behavior that she began in college fifteen years ago. Without tasting it, she wolfs down the candy and feels sick and hateful the next day. The night before our session, she reports she did something uncharacteristic: she wanted to eat, but didn't.

"I feel different. I'm more aware of what I'm doing. I'm changing." As she says these words, Lisa turns her head to the right and presses it back so that she no longer faces directly toward me. A sophisticated student of therapy, she notices her gesture immediately, exaggerates her behavior, and creates her own experiment. She pulls her head further to the right and back, and says, "I'm anxious and embarrassed.

You won't approve of me, and I need you to."

"Are you sure?" I ask.

Lisa looks surprised, "No, you're not my parent, and I'm not a child."

Lisa is seated. I place two wooden blocks under her feet, five inches high, five inches deep, and nine inches wide. "Sense the press of your feet onto the blocks," I tell her, "with your hands resting on the arm rests, and say the words, 'I'm different. I'm changing.'" She begins to do so and with every repetition of the phrase, her head wanders off to the side, or her chin drops to her chest, or her forehead raises. Her expression is anxious and lacks support. The words tumble out of her mouth and onto her lap. She laughs at her inability to say the phrase directly. "That's comical! I used to hate myself when I did any of these things. Now I can laugh."

I realize the split between Lisa's intention—to make her statement with clarity and directly to me—and her behavior. "Yes, you're changing," I say, "and you need to support your new experience." I invite Lisa to experiment with a developmental movement pattern. To demonstrate, I stand several inches in front of the wall and place the palm of each hand, shoulder height and shoulder width, in front of me. I invite Lisa to do the same. As in the prior experiment while she was seated in the chair, I ask her to sense her feet pushing onto the floor; the floor pressing up and into her feet; her hands pushing into the wall; and the wall pressing into her hands. She reports that she feels the floor under her, but that she cannot discern her hands upon the wall. I adjust the experiment. She flexes at her wrists, which pulls both her palms and fingers off the wall. Having done this, she stretches the skin of each palm and slowly places her hands, making a rolling motion from wrist to finger, onto the wall. To further emphasize the connection between her palm and the wall, I pull and lengthen each of her fingers and gently press her knuckles down. "I'm feeling my hands, and now I have a better sense of my feet on the floor," she reports.

Lisa breathes deeply. For a few moments her head balances above an elongated spine, but then her body drifts forward, and she rests her head on the wall. She is no longer standing on her own two feet. I bring her attention to this postural adjustment. "I didn't notice that I moved forward. I do feel comfortable leaning here. I feel some sort of relief." I encourage her to continue leaning and to notice where in her body she senses relief. When she feels finished, I direct her to push her hands onto the wall until she stands upright. Once she rights herself, I instruct her to lean forward and to rest her head against the wall. She does, and explores the boundary between leaning onto something for support and standing on her own. After a thorough investigation of both patterns, she announces, "I think I'll rely on my legs to hold me up."

We move away from the wall and Lisa faces me. She notices that her head feels "lighter and more balanced," and says that she feels energy "streaming through my hands and my legs." With greater supports in place, I ask her to persist and to repeat her words, "I'm changing." She struggles with the statement. Her expression does not feel "genuine" to her, she says. "Be aware of your body," I say. "Let me be only peripheral to your experience. Sense where in *your* body that you know you're changing." After making several more attempts, Lisa feels the authenticity of her words. Quite spontaneously, she says, "Ruella, *I* know I've changed." This time, she includes me in her experience. She smiles and laughs.

Several Weeks Later

Sitting upright and easily aligned, Lisa reports that she is feeling "really good." On a number of occasions, she has chosen not to binge. She is better focused at work and is more attentive to her family. She has not "felt this good for a really long time," she says. I ask her what she might like to do with the hour and she quickly answers, "Moving would be good. I'd like to do something with my feet or hands."

Lisa tells me that she took a long walk the other night and noticed that she could not relax her hands, and that her legs felt as though they might give out on her. I invite her to lie down on her back. When she does, I sit by her feet and to the side of her. Slowly, and with her permission, I place one hand at the back of her ankle and the other at the back of her knee. I rotate her leg inward and lift it toward her chest. Once her leg is in a flexed position, I rotate her thigh slightly outward, and ask her to press her foot into my hand until she has straightened her leg. She presses her leg forward, and

I give her an equal measure of resistance. Once she has met the pressure of my hand and straightened her leg, I ask her to relax. Then I rotate the same leg inward, bring it toward her chest, rotate it outward, and ask her to press firmly into my hand until she has lengthened her leg once more. We repeat this movement several times.

At first, I hardly feel Lisa's foot push into my hand, and I encourage her to press between her toe-ball and the front of her heel bone. As she exerts more force, she rotates her head to the side, tenses her jaw, arches her low spine off the floor, and hyper-extends her fingers. It takes us many tries with both her legs until she has found the appropriate coordination of hip, leg, and foot so that she can meet my resistance and complete the task. The movement is not easy for her. She cannot sense *her* feet while pressing into *my* hand.

The experiment is diagnostic, and it demonstrates *how* and *where* Lisa interrupts the clarity of a fluid pushing pattern. It seems impossible for her to push her leg into my hand without tensing her neck, jaw, low back, and even her fingers. I devise another experiment that will give her the sufficient support to work through these inhibited coordinations more easily. I ask her to sit in front of the wall and press both feet onto it. I sit behind her, press my back into hers, and place the soles of my feet on the floor directly in front of my hips. When she feels my back against hers, I ask Lisa to press both her feet onto the wall and push toward me. Lisa tries the experiment several times. "I don't want to overpower you," she says. "How would you know if you were overpowering me?" I ask. She cannot answer. I suggest that she pay close attention to her experience. When she is more keenly aware of her body, she will be able to sense whether or not she overpowers me.

She pushes harder onto the wall, and I feel the muscles of her back activate. I respond in kind; I push my feet onto the floor and my back into hers. We both play at this boundary, giving and taking from one another. She pushes into me. My firm resisting supplies her leverage. I push into her. She makes her back a stable and reliable support. When we both feel finished, we stand and face each other. "I can feel all of me face you . . . from back to front," she says with some excitement. I ask her to take her time while she meets the whole of her self. We breathe deeply.

Lisa decides that she would like to walk around the room. Her first few steps are bold and fluid. Her head floats easily above her neck. But within moments I observe, and she notices, her hands tense and extend and her head begins to drift sidewards. We settle back into the big green armchairs to explore what has just taken place. "The same thing happened on my walk," she says, "I had twenty more minutes until I could get back home, and I was in a panic because my legs wouldn't support me. I didn't think I could make it. I was gripping my abdomen and tensing my hands."

I think aloud and tell Lisa that children who have to suppress their longing for their mothers often become independent prematurely. Without feeling rooted to their mothers, they have difficulty rooting to the earth and don't feel completely secured on their legs. Lisa says nothing, and I hold my breath, wondering whether my spontaneous narrative was useful. Then, Lisa says she is aware that the toes of both her feet flex upward as her wrists flex and her fingers extend. I invite her to follow the movement. When she does, both her legs contract onto the seat of the chair and into her torso, while the soles of her feet face me. Simultaneously, both her arms contract into her chest, and her palms face toward me.

"What do you want to do now?" I ask. Quickly, she springs forward, stomps both feet on the ground, and pushes her hands toward me. "I *don't* want to *hear* that [my story]," she says, quite spontaneously. Startled by her statement, she flexes into a ball once more, springs forward, repeats the movement, and says, "I *don't* want to *feel* that." Again, she is surprised by her response. "When I say *no* to you, I feel myself," she says. We sit for a while impressed with the clarity of her statement. "You seemed so determined when you said no," I tell her. "Yes, I felt determined, and I think I felt angry. I felt good, but then I just shrank," she says.

We decide that Lisa might need to practice getting to know her "*no*," and she continues to experiment with her lively movement pattern. After several more attempts, she is able to push, to say the words, and to feel her angry determination. The pattern completes itself. We feel satisfied.

I ask Lisa to stand and face me, pushing her feet onto the floor and pushing her hands toward me. Then I ask her to say, "You're over there." I now instruct her to place both hands on her chest and repeat, "I'm over here." Lisa enjoys the experiment. "You're over there, and I'm over here," she says and repeats the motion and the words several times. Standing on her own two feet, her head balanced evenly atop her spine, she reports, "I really see you now!" "Wonderful!" I say, "I'd hate you to miss such an object of beauty." Lisa laughs. "Now I *know* we're different. I would *never* say *that*."

Psychodynamics

Lisa's early upbringing was organized around her relationship with two depressed and very demanding parents. Her "job" was to make them happy so that they might, in turn, give Lisa the approval and support she wanted. The dynamic has left her constantly conforming to the wants and needs of others in order to gain their favor. She easily gives up on what she wants most, and gives her self away.

The continual suppression and frustration of her appetites and her real desires leave Lisa with an intense craving. She misinterprets her longing and frequently binges on candy; the background and more profound need, the longing for nurturance and comfort, lingers. The inner emptiness of this greater loss is not fully experienced.

Lisa's previous therapy has heightened awareness of her symbiotic behaviors as they emerge within our relational dyad. In the years we have worked together, she has moved from the confusion and vagueness of a dependent, confluent style to the greater clarity of herself *and* me. She now catches herself behaving in ways that are meant to gain my approval, and sometimes she can feel the disdain that underlies her constant self-sacrifice. Still, the pattern of collapsing, especially when she is angry, and the loss of herself to another are apparent within her upright stance. Her head does not clarify her intentions, her legs do not support her spine easily and her spine does not support the manipulations of her arms.

At the beginning of the first session described here, Lisa repeatedly lost herself to me. She could not state the *rightness* of her experience—"*I feel different, I'm changing*"—without worrying. This was made obvious by the movements of her head to the side and back. To heighten awareness, I propped her feet with blocks. The props pressed into her limbs, stimulating sensations at her periphery, and gave subtle feedback to her spine, reducing excess muscular tension. The lessened strain increased Lisa's bodily sensations. She could notice *how* she avoided her excitement in my presence.

In the wall experiment, the tensions of Lisa's shoulders, neck, and head interrupted the energetic experience of her hands meeting the wall. To release the excess tension, she stretched both her hands onto the wall. I pulled and lengthened her fingers to further heighten her proprioceptive responses.

This experiment was based on the developmental righting and pushing patterns. The infant on her belly lifts her head while pressing onto the floor to support the weight of her torso. The pattern organizes the differentiation of the infant's head/spine, limbs/spine, and front/back. It also differentiates the infant from that which she presses onto and with. Clear feedback from Lisa's hands pushing onto the wall stimulated a kinetic chain beginning with her hands, and then traveling through her arms, shoulders, collarbones, downward to her breastbone, ribs, and continuing around to her spine and head. A clarity in energetic connection allowed her spine to lengthen, while the muscles of her shoulders softened and realigned. Her head was now freed to center on her neck. In response, Lisa experienced the weight of her body on her feet.

Not yet emotionally able to support the novelty of the shift, an unaware Lisa drifted forward and rested her head onto the wall. A primary conflict was brought into awareness: *how/when do I need to support myself; how/when do I need to rely on "you?"* When Lisa brought herself upright, the effort that was required to execute this pushing movement stimulated her healthy and often inhibited aggression. Organismic integrity prevailed, and she chose to stand on her own two feet.

Lisa faced me and reiterated the phrase that opened our session: "I feel different. I'm changing." Although she had the greater support of a more balanced stance, the newness of her experience was too strange for her to tolerate, and she quickly shut down her excitement. She was not able to look at me and simultaneously feel her own body. I realized that her sensori-receptive system dominated and overpowered her proprioception: I appeared too large in her experience. I then directed Lisa's attention to her sensations: "Be aware of your body. Let me be peripheral." With this minor yet necessary support from me, Lisa experienced her self. Her authentic expression emerged.

Several weeks later, we experimented with her lower extremities. I realized that the flexor/extension patterns of her legs had neither been fully developed nor assimilated into her upright pattern. I created an experiment based on the early infant reactions of *flexor withdrawal* and *extensor thrust*.[2] The experiment was intended to investigate the earlier supports for Lisa's walking experiences. From these basic movements, more varied patterns of flexion and extension evolve.

As Lisa performed the movements, it became obvious that it was difficult for her to thrust her foot, leg, and thigh into my hand with confidence. In order to hold back a healthy aggressive movement of her limbs, she tensed the muscles of her neck, jaw, and low spine. Even her fingers participated in the struggle. The experiment was diagnostic. Lisa learned *how* and *where* she held herself back.

I created a different experiment intended to lend more support to her spine, while differentiating her spine from her lower limbs. This experiment was derived from another variation of developmental pattern: while on his back, the infant pushes one or both feet onto the floor, which lifts his pelvis and stimulates his back muscles.

When Lisa and I sat back to back, she was able to feel the press of her feet onto the wall. Like the infant's pushing pattern of feet onto the floor, a movement reaction was stimulated from each of her feet through the joints of her ankles, knees, and hip sockets. The deep, flexor muscles along either side of her spine (the psoas) activated and supported her pushing. When Lisa relinquished her perpetual worry about overpowering another, she found the simplicity of her healthy and determined thrust. This was as much energy as was necessary to complete her movement, and not more.

Lisa stood and experienced herself completely, "from front to back." Her head balanced easily on her neck. When she walked around the room, however, she swiftly interrupted her upright and forthright expression. Her routinized and tedious tensional pattern returned. She described having taken a long walk in which her limbs had felt unreliable, and she had panicked. As I listened, I imagined a young girl, alone in the woods and terrified. I shared my thoughts about children who were forced to become independent too soon. Lisa listened and responded through the language of her body: flexed hands and feet.

When I encouraged her to follow through with her stunted movement impulses, she flexed her limbs into her body and then swiftly extended them. She pushed toward me with the strength and support of her whole being. The experiment was executed with an appropriate aggressive effort. Energy that was generally pooled at the center of her body moved fluidly to the periphery, her hands and feet. The release of the excess tension held at the spine allowed her head to naturally right itself. With repetition, the anger that accompanied the pattern emerged. Lisa stood, faced me, and pushed toward me once more. This time she asserted, "You're over there," and with a hand on her chest, ". . . and I'm over here." The clarity of the pattern along with her words reinforced the clarity of our relationship.

In this vignette, the somatic/developmental patterns were used in a variety of ways to help encourage Lisa's upright and autonomous experience. These sessions were particularly important to her growth. Lisa has become much more authentic in her dealings with others, and is now more capable of holding onto her own experience when directly encountering another.

Karen

Karen's head presses forward while the base of her neck simultaneously contracts backward. The ambivalence of the pattern creates acute tension in the muscles of her neck and shoulders. The resulting stress reverberates down the length of her spinal column and causes spasticity, especially in her upper back. Her arm movements are inhibited by the stuck position of her shoulder blades, which appear to be glued to the sides of her rib cage. The strain in her shoulder area also affects the muscles of her throat.

Karen has great difficulty meeting others; she repetitively reaches out and holds back. This constant interrupted dialogue creates a muscular rigidity that is revealed throughout her entire body and powerfully distorts her upright stance. Her withheld aggression creates spasms in her spinal column, obstructs her potential to reach out, and further inhibits her expressive action. Her movements are tentative and underscore her distrust of both her own behaviors and those of others. The overall pattern of her bound efforts reveals a healthy aggression turned inward. With so much excitement mounting and immediately being withheld, Karen is deeply frustrated. Her blocked energy creates a constant backdrop of discomfort that diverts her from a more profound suffering. Her discomfort is, however, not focused, and she is in an interminable state of undifferentiated distress; at any given time, she can agonize about almost anything.

The rigid holding in her head, neck, and shoulders forces Karen to move these areas as if they were a single piece. This tense muscular upper body pattern closes her throat, and leaves her with only the trickle of a whine. Paralleling the constrictions of her throat, separate tensions gather in the area of her abdomen. When she cries, she habitually tenses her throat and her belly even more, which interferes with the fullness of her experience.

Further restrictions are also apparent in Karen's lower body. The muscles of her low back tighten and exaggerate the subtle curve of her spine. Her inner thigh muscles also contract, and pull her upper legs together. In addition, the tension pattern of her calves and shins is so powerful that her lower legs rotate inward and bow backward. These distortions prevent the weight of her body from easily transferring downward and into the earth. As if in contradiction to the energetic thrust of her legs and thighs, which moves upward, creating constriction at each of her hip sockets, her feet collapse and roll inward. From all directions, powerful energetic constraints are held near her body's center, while the periphery, her hands and feet, remain weakened. It is little wonder that Karen has a difficult time standing her ground.

Karen: In a Workshop Seminar

At the beginning of this teaching seminar, I ask the group what they hope to derive from the week-long training, both professionally and personally. This first introduction allows me to know something about each person, as well as to experience myself in relation to him or her. My first reactions to each student are crucial and tell me something about both of us. Generally, these impressions are confirmed as the week-long intensive continues.

In this first "go-around," Karen introduces herself and announces, "I really want to have fun. That's why I came." She says this with a big smile and looking straight at me. Immediately, my shoulders and jaw tense. A challenging task is already in the making. I must show Karen a good time. I file her request and my experience away . . . for the moment.

Three Days into the Seminar

Karen sits across from me, stretching her neck. She bends it from side to side, pushes it forward to her chest, brings it back up, and makes small half-circles with her head from one shoulder to the other. I bring her attention to her movements. "I'm testing when I feel pain and when I don't," she says, and continues to experiment. Voicing what I imagine is her experience, I say, "Sometimes I'm in pain and sometimes I'm not." Karen grins, "Oh, no. I'm in pain *all* the time."

Struck by the incongruence of her statement and her smile, I ask her to experiment. "Would you repeat this sentence, 'Ruella, I want you to know I'm in pain all the time,' and do so without your smile?" Karen makes the statement. She feels the weight of her words, appears sad and withdraws. In the silence of her melancholy, her feet shuffle. I breathe deeply and wait.

Karen glances downward and notices the movement of her feet. Seemingly out of nowhere, she says, "I hate my feet." Again she grows silent. I wait. As if talking to herself, she relates a story of a recent skiing adventure. "I fell flat on my face," she says, smiling, "I think my neck became much worse." I respond, "You punctuate your most important statements with a smile. I feel the seriousness of your experience, yet you diminish the importance of your expression." Karen's eyes fill with tears, "I really hurt my neck." I answer, "I believe you."

Karen cries, then abruptly stops. We both notice the process by which she holds herself back. She tightens her abdomen, presses her head further forward, clenches her jaw, and tenses her throat, neck, and shoulders, all of which prevent her from breathing easily. "Now my neck is *really* in pain." Frustrated with herself once more, Karen says, "Why can't I let go?" I ask her to experiment with the words, "I have to hold myself back just now. I'm not sure why." Karen repeats the sentence and clearly is miserable in the process: "Urrgghh. I sound like I'm whining." Her head presses even further forward, and her shoulders elevate.

Feeling the depth of her frustration, and the beginning of my own stiff neck, I slow my breathing and feel the chair under me. Once I am sure exactly what *I* feel, I direct my attention to her. "Karen, you're in a bind. You hurt. When you tell me directly, you hate yourself. When you disguise your need, you hurt even more. You are in a no-win situation."

Karen looks down. Her eyes fill. This time she does nothing to interrupt her tears. I feel relieved. "I'm thinking of my mother," she says, "She's very difficult." Karen cries deeply, then comes the expected, self-deprecating remark: "I don't like to talk about my mother and cry. I want to talk about her and *not* cry." Karen has successfully turned her anger inward once more. Speaking *for* her and with a different perspective, I say, "Sometimes I cry when I speak of my mother, and sometimes I get angry." Delighted to have been understood, Karen says, "Yes, that's true! I like that." I add the statement, "And sometimes when I speak of my mother, I cry even though I'm really *angry*." She repeats the sentence directly to me and with ease. "You're right. I never realized that before." This time there is no self-recrimination to diminish her experience.

I ask Karen if her mother was in a similar bind—often frustrated and angry with herself. "Yes, most of the time. I'm different," she says. She eagerly lists how she and her mother are separate people. "I don't inflict my bad moods on anyone. I'm more aware of my behaviors. I'm a better mother to my children. Well, at least now I am . . . some of the time, anyway." Karen begins reducing her excitement. "Sometimes I'm a better mother and sometimes I'm not," I add. Karen straightens herself in the chair, and her face brightens, "I feel good when I hear you say I don't have to be different all the time. I feel easier in my body. My shoulders don't hurt."

I notice that Karen's head aligns with her torso and her voice sounds deeper and more resonant. Several of the workshop participants spontaneously confirm this fact. I ask Karen if she would share her newly discovered vocal strength with the group members. When she faces the group, Karen immediately presses her head forward, tenses her throat, and loses the power of her voice.

One member recalls an experiment of the prior afternoon, when Karen threw a ball as part of a group/reaching experiment. During that experiment, the group observes, she did not throw the ball directly toward the other person. Further, she threw underhand, and when she was asked to experiment with an overhand throw, she became anxious. "It might be too forceful," she said. The group had devised an experiment. Instead of standing and throwing the ball to someone, Karen sat on the floor and rolled the ball toward the other. As she experimented with a "grounded" pathway, she was able to better control the ball's speed. The movement experiment provided her the support to express herself directly and with enough force to reach another person. Vocalizing, however, is a more difficult matter for her.

Now, I suggest to Karen that we experiment again with the ball and in a different way. She seems curious and excited. I tell her to place the twelve-inch, round ball between her thighs and squeeze it. She does so. Instantly, she startles with surprise and amusement: "Oh my god! I really feel my legs and feet. They're so solid! And my voice—it's booming. I feel powerful!" I also notice that her shoulders have released, her upper chest has widened along her collarbones, and her head has once again realigned.

I tell her to share some of her power with the group. "Squeeze the ball, feel the strength of your legs, and tell them how different you are from your mother." With excitement, Karen meets each member of the group and shares her new-found power. When she gets to the final member, Mark, she hesitates. "He looks as if he's not interested." "Does it really matter?" I ask. She smiles, "Mark, I'm different from my mother, even if you don't care." Turning to me she adds, "I like that. I don't have to care what Mark thinks." "Karen," I say, "you don't even have to care what your mother thinks." Laughing, Karen removes the ball, continues to feel the power of her legs under her, and with full voice, declares, "Mother, I don't care what you think!"

Psychodynamics

Infants and children who have lived with ongoing traumas throughout their upbringing have difficulty moving smoothly through the sequences of development. As adults, they lack sufficient background supports for healthy contacting: postural stability and balance; proprioceptive awareness; and coordinated movements.

In Karen's childhood, she had to continually suppress her excitements to conform to her parents' needs, especially those of her mother. Unable to experience and express her differences from her mother, she became thwarted in her natural progression toward autonomy. When she did express herself, she lived in fear of criticism/humiliation. With repetition, she learned to doubt her own impulses and to diminish her own authority. In times of stress her impulses to negate herself became stronger. Eventually, her "no" turned inward and provided a terrible yet reliable sense of stability. At the same time, to deny her authenticity made her furious. With no way to express the intensity of her hatred, she hated herself.

As an adult, Karen still finds it dangerous to express her genuine anger. Instead it emerges as a list of complaints, mostly about herself. Contained within her grievances is an intense longing for comfort, compassion, and love. Although her complaints are an attempt to garner some kind of support, they seem only to stimulate further frustration, in her and often in others.

Throughout the session, I observed the familiar rhetorical style by which Karen inhibited her experience. Through a series of experimental reframings, I offered her alternative ways to venture out of her rigid fixation. These interventions shifted her habitual experience, though not for long. Embedded within the spasticity and tension of her energetic system, an internalized and critical, parental voice continued to express itself.

Throwing a ball is parallel to throwing one's voice. But Karen needed more supports in place to reach the group members with her words. I intuitively chose to work with her lower extremities, which were far less traumatized than the region of her head and neck and so more available. The task of squeezing the ball between her thighs captured Karen's attention. In the act: her legs and feet realigned; her pelvic muscles released; and the psoas muscles along the front of the spine that are so crucial to upright support were stimulated. More easily balanced and with a lessening of muscular tension, Karen could better experience herself on the earth.

With the supports of her lower body in place, the substantial constrictions of Karen's upper spine, shoulders, neck, and throat could lessen, and her head balanced more evenly on her spine. Her generally constricted aggression moved outward. She became an active agent in defining her experience. She asserted herself, and with humor. Karen felt "powerful."

* * *

The somatic/developmental interventions that were used within Lisa's and Karen's therapy stimulated formerly inhibited neuromuscular connections. With both clients, the novel pattern flowed from the periphery, the sensory organs and limbs, and moved sequentially to the center, the spinal column. The movement was completed simply and gracefully, by the most direct route, and with the least expenditure of effort.

Whenever a developmental imbalance is firmly organized, or fixed, it modifies the earlier and the later patterns that are to emerge. This was true for each client, as distortions in righting influenced and inhibited her pushing. I chose experiments that addressed and strengthened pushing experiences for both. Once these later patterns were stimulated into sharp awareness, the underlying righting pattern emerged with greater clarity. Immediately, a change in psychic organization became evident. Both Lisa and Karen came to experience their upright selves in the face of another.

Chapter Five Notes
The Upright Stance

1. L. Bly, *The Components of Normal Movement during the First Year of Life* (Chicago: Neuro-Developmental Treatment Association, 1983).

2. Flexor withdrawal and extensor thrust are reactions that underlie and support the infant's ability to both withdraw from and push toward the other. In flexor withdrawal, the infant's leg is extended. When the sole of its foot is stimulated, the infant withdraws the leg inward into a full flexion pattern. The reaction underlies all total flexion movements of the leg emanating from the foot, for example, kicking, and later, walking. In extensor thrust, the infant's leg is flexed. When the sole of the foot is stimulated, the infant pushes the stimulant away and, thereby, extends the leg. The reaction underlies all total extension movements of the leg that are emanating from the foot, for example, kicking, and later, walking.

Chapter Six

෪

Coming Into Wholeness: Annie's Story

While previous chapters have focused upon the function of one or more infant patterns and their use within a therapy session, it is now time to demonstrate how developmental patterns work in concert within long-term therapy. This chapter is devoted to one client, Annie, and our therapy work over time.

I was in my third year of Gestalt training and practice, when Annie and I began therapy. At the time, I had no idea how much she would influence both my work and my life. While she was one of my most challenging clients, she was also a person whom I grew to dearly love. Her sincere desire to work through her difficulties, as well as her willingness to explore, allowed me to test a variety of somatic and developmental experiments within our sessions. These ongoing investigations deeply influenced our therapy and affirmed for me that I was on the right path in pursuing my somatic developmental approach.

The chapter begins with a detailed physical description of Annie at the beginning of our work together. To know how she carries herself and moves through her world gives the reader the opportunity to kinesthetically and empathetically attune to her experience. The portrayal also sensitizes us to the subtleties in Annie's behavior, for example, the tensing of her jaw or the contraction of her shoulders, which become the basis for psychological explorations. I have also offered the reader a subsequent description of Annie at the completion of her therapy. This later depiction demonstrates how the shifts in her psychological experience are reflected in the many changes in her physical processes.

As I have provided a developmental framework throughout this book, it is important for the reader to know that the therapy is not implemented sequentially. It is clearly seen here that the therapist does not begin with the first infant pattern to develop and proceed to apply each successive pattern to the client. At the same time that somatic and developmental patterns provide an under-standing of human development, they comprise the phenomenology of the present. *The therapist becomes aware of the client's most obvious psychological concern and its attendant sensorimotor correlates, the developmental patterns, as they emerge in the ongoing context of the psychotherapy session.* The reader will further understand that it is not important for the therapist to interpret what happened in the client's infancy by "fitting" his or her behaviors into a developmental frame. Provided with an overall knowledge of the infant's somatic development, the therapist creates the most appropriate experiment, and the client arrives at his or her own experiential interpretation.

Each of the varied experiments we did helped Annie develop supports for fluid contacting. The blocks and obstructions to her healthy self could not have been reached or worked through with such success with out the integration of this developmental approach. My understanding of developmental patterns helped to clarify several of Annie's behaviors that would otherwise have remained mysterious. Further, experimenting from a somatic and developmental framework enabled me to discover parts of Annie that could easily have been overlooked or dismissed, and crucial facets of her self would not have been addressed.

The outcome of any therapy relies upon a successful relationship between therapist and client. When Annie and I experimented with a diversity of patterns, the opportunities for a variety of relational experiences opened. We came to know one another while sitting opposite each other in chairs; while we were seated together on the floor; as she lay across a large gymnastic ball and I held onto her; when she curled into a fetal-like position and I sat next to her; and as we stood and faced each other. This multiplicity of relational explorations created continual shifts in the ways we experienced ourselves and each other. As our relationship evolved, it was possible to deepen the somatic work. And, the deeper somatic work helped to strengthen our therapy alliance.

The case presentations within other chapters have been written to highlight particular developmental patterns and their relationship to each client's somatic processes. Annie's story is written at a broader level. It demonstrates how a solid background in somatic development deepens the therapist's fundamental understanding of her client. In it, the reader will see how our therapy dyad, while not always smooth or graceful, developed the kind of flexibility and resilience out of which a successful outcome emerges.

The following is based on my recollections of our earliest meetings and my detailed notes. It begins with Annie, in 1985.

Annie, 1985

Annie stands in the office vestibule and removes her shoes. She is an attractive large-boned woman with deep blue eyes and waist-length black hair. She lifts her head to briefly look my way and then plows, head-first, into the room. Her stride is both determined and awkward.

When she is seated across from me, I notice that the muscles of her neck constrict and form a thickened column. The muscular tension, most obvious along the sides of her throat, creates an energetic separation between her head and torso. I also observe tension at the base of her skull and the base of her neck. These chronic contractions shorten the muscles of her neck and intensify its spinal curve.

Annie's shoulders are broad and solid, and her rib cage is wide, with the bottom ribs slightly flared. Her upper arm bones rotate inward in their sockets and produce a slight rounding. While the top of her breastbone presses toward her spine and backward, her lower ribs lift upward. It is as if a hand presses on her upper chest and pushes her backward. So as not to be a pushover, Annie counterbalances by pressing her defiant lower ribs forward and up.

Standing up, Annie rotates her pelvis forward which exaggerates the curve of her low spine. The pelvic rotation stiffens the muscles of her lower back and disrupts a substantial support from the deeper skeletal muscles along the front of the spine. So much energy is given over to holding herself tight and erect that Annie cannot sense, let alone, use these deeper muscles to support her. The shortening of muscles at both her low back and the base of her neck pull Annie backward, while the lift of her lower ribs presses her up and out. Her postural pattern expresses a confused and conflicted intention: *do I approach or do I avoid?* All these tensions do not allow a smooth side-to-side swing of her pelvis as she moves. Instead, her walk is reserved and held.

Because Annie's pelvis is misaligned, it cannot rest and balance lightly upon the two heads of the thighbones. This creates a lack of freedom in each hip socket and a subsequent inhibition of pelvic movements. In addition, the muscles of Annie's inner thighs constrict, while the outer seams appear weakened.

The misalignment of both thighs to the pelvis interrupts gravity's downward flow from the sacral joints, through the center of either hip socket, the center of each knee, the fronts of the ankles, and onto the earth. This places the weight of Annie's body toward the back of her heels.

To balance, she must lock her kneecaps and grip her legs. The bones of her thick ankles fall subtly inward, weakening her arches. The over-development of the front of her thighs, the gripping of her legs and ankles, and the weakened support from her feet do not permit Annie to clearly sense the earth beneath her. She presses ahead without sufficient foundation. Because her gait is resolute, it lacks spring and the lightness of play.

The determined quality of Annie's movements resides uneasily on an overall dense muscular tone. From this underlying flow of tension, she approaches others with caution. In her hesitancy, in fact, she sometimes moves against others rather than toward them. When she feels excited, the increase to her muscular tension causes her to fidget. Her thoughts wander. When the excitement is prolonged, she becomes agitated and increasingly apprehensive. She obsesses. With so much unaware energy held tight in her body's tissues, she feels generally anxious and depressed.

Annie's eyes are often cast downward, and they seldom meet mine. Sometimes, when she does look in my direction, she glares. This look of camouflaged suspicion is mirrored in the set of her recalcitrant jaw, which is pulled in and upward. Her facial expressions comment on everything with a wince, a painful grimace, with eye rolling, raised eyebrows or a pout. Every feeling that passes through her body is exaggerated by the muscles of her face. Her expressions are a continual litany of criticisms about herself, primarily, or others. To look at her, it would appear as if nothing is hidden. In reality, everything is hidden.

Annie's gestures are as varied as her moods. When she is troubled, they can be small and tight, like the methodical twisting of a tissue she holds in her hands. If her disturbance is prolonged, her gestures become tighter and more bound, and soon they explode. When she feels optimistic, her gestures are graceful, and they pinpoint the direction in which they choose to go. They are executed with vigor and resolve. In moments of dramatic despair, Annie's gestures lose this precision of direction and have a quality of indulgence, a giving in to the grandeur of expression.

I see that Annie's breathing pattern is habitually irregular. She forces air in, and holds onto her inhalation by gripping her abdominal muscles. On the following exhale, her air rushes out. The complete pattern is: an energetic inhale executed with too much effort; holding on to what she has just taken in (the gripped abdominal area); and finally gushing out.

This rhythmic imbalance reflects two different styles of managing stress. For one, when Annie feels threatened, she moves swiftly to emergency mode and prepares to fight or flee. She then holds her inhalation even longer. The extended inflation expands her upper torso and she seems bigger. But holding on to her air leads to a disturbing apprehension: she feels the approaching edge of fragmentation and then rages. These anxious rages are turned against someone else and, of course, turned against her. Gripped at the top of her inhalation, Annie is suspended, and with no relief in sight.

The other way Annie deals with perceived danger is to collapse and become paralyzed. At these moments, she lives as if she cannot rise to the demands of the situation. She eats compulsively, watches hours of television, and simultaneously reads. She is unable to perform even the most basic of caretaking functions. Sadly, she sits at the bottom of her exhalation, lacking the requisite energy with which to fill herself.

With such disruption in her basic supports, the spontaneous and creative life that Annie longs for becomes a struggle, and most often an impossibility. She is disoriented, and therefore isolated and estranged even in her closest relationships. She holds on tight, yet falls apart at the slightest provocation. She is unsure of going forward and cannot pull away. Somewhere in her development, Annie learned that it was dangerous to "be."

Our Early Sessions

Annie was referred to me by her friend, who was one of my clients. She knew that I "worked with the body" and said she was particularly interested in that aspect of our therapy because she had always felt "uncomfortable" in her own skin. Within the first weeks of our working together, she requested that we do some kind of bodywork. While she was unsure of exactly what she had in mind, she said she knew that she wanted to lie down. I placed a yoga mat on the floor and Annie lay on her back. When I sat next to her, she immediately became disconcerted and said she felt as though she were falling. I noticed a subtle backward movement of her head as she grasped onto the sides of the mat. The front of her torso flexed, as did her upper thighs.

Although at the time I had no clear understanding of what I was observing, I had the good sense to have Annie roll onto her side, push her hands onto the floor, and bring herself to a seated posture. As she levered herself upright, awareness of her body-weight sensations heightened. Now she was present. We moved back to our chairs, and we remained there for the next several years of our sessions. Hereafter, any sensorimotor work was done in the upright position. It was not until I had a deeper understanding of infant development and Gestalt psychotherapy that I realized what had occurred.

Lying belly up, and with me sitting next to her, Annie had inadvertently made herself far too vulnerable. We had not yet developed a reliable, consistent and, therefore supportive enough relationship for her to risk exposure. To relax on one's back often elicits some quality of falling. This is particularly true if a person has held on so tightly that the extensor muscles along the back of the spine have become stiff. When these muscles begin to release, the person feels the weight of his or her bones *land* on the earth. Annie's extensor muscles released, and she perceived herself falling. What rushed forward was her intense fear of letting go, and the accompanying, deep-rooted belief, still out of her awareness, of what happens when one surrenders to another. Annie felt as if the ground had moved out from under her, and she startled. Her habitual underlying pattern of organization, the sensation that she was always on shaky ground, emerged. To control these sensations, she contracted the muscles along the front of her body and grasped the mat for support.

Her reaction was reminiscent of the Moro, the young infant's response to a sudden loss of support, which integrates into the developing nervous system and becomes the startle response. If the infant or child's sense of safety has been threatened too frequently and with too great an intensity, continual startles become shocks to the nervous system. These acute episodes are punctuated by low-level and chronic dangers and frustrations for which the child is constantly preparing. If the child does not learn to release the repetitive jolts to her system, she becomes traumatized—a result of their accumulation. The traumatic experience is inscribed within the child's neuromuscular organization and, unless it is addressed, continues throughout adulthood.

Much later, I wondered if Annie's request for the bodywork experiment had been expressing a formerly unfulfilled and persistent need. Perhaps she had wanted to feel safe and cared for as she lay on her back and looked up at me. This perceptual/relational configuration evoked a primary caregiving experience that had been interrupted early on. Neither I nor anyone could give back what had been taken away from Annie, nor would it have been appropriate to try. Nevertheless, Annie could learn to make herself safe in a variety of relational configurations with me, and then with others.

For now, however, Annie was unable to let go, to yield, and held either herself tight or collapsed. In neither position could she sense her body nor experience the other with any clarity. She had numerous symptoms that were a product of this fear of surrender. The hypertension of her extensor muscles had become a continual problem, and she suffered from low-back, neck, and shoulder pains. The tension in the base of her skull was also noticeable in the severe gripping of her jaw. The pattern was especially evident when she became anxious. And when she was angry, clenching and gripping her jaw fused with her anger; in fact, it was impossible for her to feel angry without the accompanying response of clenching. This gripped pattern caused her to grind her teeth, sometimes during the day and particularly at night.

When Annie felt threatened, she was thrown off balance. At these times, she described a feeling of shakiness in her legs. She was convinced that her legs would not hold her up and that she would collapse in a pile. We often experience sensations of losing balance in the genitals. Annie contracted her thighs in an attempt to cut off genital excitation. Her need to express the excitement conflicted with a need to constrict and hold herself in and back. She could neither fully release her excitation, nor still it.[1]

Finally, Annie had a long standing problem with overeating and weekly bingeing and, at one time, she had been bulimic. Her desperate longing was organized around a constant hunger and the search for just the right taste. Annie ate until she literally bloated. For the moment, her craving was muted.

The Therapy: 1985-1996

Annie's early life was filled with loss, trauma, and the ongoing dangers and frustrations that come from living in a family desperately in need of comfort, but not knowing how to find it. Each family member never knew how to say what he or she wanted. And, because they were unable to say it, they never really knew what it was. The terrifying and incestuous demands of Annie's stepfather and stepbrother manifested their desire to be close, acted out in twisted and disturbed behaviors.[2]

Her mother, overwhelmed and depressed from the loss of her first husband, and then her beloved son, was filled with unexpressed regrets. The abandonment by a mother lost to her own despair was stitched into the fabric of Annie's being. Annie became the bearer of her mother's tragedies. In her loyalty, the unspoken contract was signed: Mother, if you have regrets, I cannot exist.

My early experiences of working with Annie were not easy. This was especially true in moments of her rage. In one session I had been rubbing the face of my wristwatch, which I held in one hand. From what seemed to me out of nowhere, Annie snapped at me, "Could you please stop doing that, it's annoying," and then proceeded to devalue me and my work. I felt my shoulders tense, my throat constrict, and my diaphragm freeze. I was angry that she had snapped at me, but held back my expression of it in the service of the therapy. My fantasy was to push a button on the edge of my chair that would eject her quietly and swiftly from my room.

It took me a while to calm down from this kind of episode, which would happen frequently during our early years, and come back to her. I gave myself a mantra, which I often repeated during such situations: "This is the best that she can do," I chanted. "If she could do any better, she would." From then on I was able to return to the session and say, "Annie, I see that you need all my attention and I do want to give it to you."

Annie was amazingly sensitive to any moment that I might wander or drift. That she perceived such subtleties of my behavior was a remarkable talent, but that she interpreted each nuance was difficult. She might react to any small movement of mine—a glance in other than her direction, a facial expression, a sigh—with feelings of fear and abandonment. She then became enraged and would attack me verbally. I learned that this gave her the feeling of control that she desperately needed to balance her feelings of loss.

This same behavior occurred in relation to her husband. When she felt abandoned and frightened, she raged at him and let herself go out of control. After this killing off, as she described it, he felt depressed and annihilated. She then felt sorry, rushed to take care of him, built him up, and felt superior to him because he was ". . . such a mess and needs me to take care of him."

When this process became more obvious through therapy, Annie began to feel her enjoyment and aliveness at her ability to "decimate" the other person. She now had the power, and she relished it. Much of her energy was invested in this process. She needed to control everything all the time. If she didn't, everyone would leave. She avoided her feelings of loss by destroying others. At the same time, she was angry that the only way to keep them around was through her exercising such control.

Her need to either control or to feel overwhelmed left her overly dependent on the other. If I (or another) gave her *everything*, she felt attended to. If there were some slight lack of coordination between the two of us, she felt enormous loss. I had to express either a constant and unconditional positive regard or she would consider me punitive. These behaviors made Annie an expert in considering her own actions or experiences to be worthless. Her well-being depended on her formidable ability to get the other to *do the right thing* while she remained passive.

Annie did not know how powerfully she could impact me or anyone else. Many times I would feed back to her how her stinging and critical remarks affected me. I would sometimes tell her that she took my breath away and admire her for her uncanny ability to cause me to freeze. These interventions worked well for both of us. Annie was always delighted to be so powerful. At the same time, I could slowly emerge from my own frozen position by sharing myself openly with her.

I would feed back any minute shift of her body or her breathing that I observed. For example, when I noticed the area of her head and neck stiffen, I would ask her to be aware of her jaw, her tongue, the back of her neck, her shoulders, and her breathing. These subtle proprioceptive awarenesses (which were akin to our more overt physical work) had a profound impact on Annie and were crucial to her healing. Similar to the processes of infant maturation, Annie needed to have a sharp awareness of her body so that she could cope with the building up of her muscular tensions in incremental doses, and thus manage the accompanying anxiety.

During these attempts to guide her into an awareness of her behaviors, Annie would sometimes feel brutally criticized. Children who feel that their parents are watching over them have the freedom to be irresponsible, but a child who feels a deep breach of faith, as Annie experienced repeatedly in her family, cannot allow herself to feel that freedom of irresponsibility. And if one cannot fully feel the healthy and necessary irresponsibility of childhood, it is difficult and painful to come into healthy adult responsibility.

To Annie, some of my interventions in session seemed like another terrible breach of faith. Once, she was so distraught and enraged with something I said that she shot up from her seat and crouched in the corner of the room behind my chair. Again, it took me a while to collect myself. I had to work through my own anxiety and anger with her behavior and my confusion as to what to do next. In such moments Annie and I had parallel experiences. This time I slowly turned to face her and saw her huddled in the corner. Immediately, I felt enormous compassion. I told her how sorry I was that I had in any way hurt her. That was never my intention. If she would come back and sit down with me, maybe we could work this out together. There was nothing that I wanted to do more than that, I said. Annie slowly moved into her chair and we found the words back to each other.

In those first few years of our working together, both Annie and I developed a deep appreciation of her view of the world: she lived as if someone were doing something to her all the time, and she wanted to "kill them for it."

Finding Ground

At the beginning of what turned out to be a long-term therapy, I began to work with Annie's inability to feel safe and surrender herself to the moment, that is, to be fully present. It was necessary for her to begin to re-experience herself as a body. Without a cohesive experience of body, she could not develop a clear and distinct self. And, experiencing her body was not possible without an awareness of her relationship to the earth.

This awareness develops in the earliest moments of life as the infant is held, picked up, rocked, cuddled, and attended to by her caregivers. When these experiences are mutually satisfying for both parties, the infant experiences a fundamental and satisfying unity of infant and environment. These moments contribute to the flowing formation of self.

Without the primary unity of oneself and the environment, great emptiness is experienced at the core of one's being. When infants or children are unable to experience their primary satisfaction of wholeness or unity with the other, they must avoid the intolerable feelings that accompany the loss. In avoiding the intolerable, they abruptly shut down their curiosity and interests.

Avoidance is the attempt to take control so that the intolerable feelings will not happen again. In the act of avoiding, proprioceptive awareness diminishes and infants or children lose a clarity of bodily sensations. They cannot differentiate themselves from the other. Both their needs and the surrounding environment become blurred. Unable to orient themselves, they become lost.

Annie and I experimented in a variety of ways to help her become more aware of herself and the ground beneath her, a *primary orienting. That* the earth could support her was a new concept for Annie. Knowing *how* she experienced support was a crucial awareness for her to cultivate. We began with what it was like for her to sit on the chair. I asked her if she could feel the weight of her body moving down into the chair and the chair pushing up to meet her. When she reported that she was unable to feel her weight or the chair clearly, I asked if she could *be* the chair. What would the chair be saying to Annie? In those experiments, the chair took on many voices. Sometimes the chair was cruel, "Go ahead, relax," it would say, "but if you do I'll pull out from under you. I won't hold you up." At other times the chair was unable to hold her. "I just can't," was its reply.

Beginning with what Annie was aware of, her back and buttocks on the chair, her feet on the ground, the background (of which she was unaware) began to surface. Her unstable relationship to the earth informed her every interest and desire. Gradually, she became aware of how she experienced what should have been a basic support in her life, the ground beneath her.

When Annie *became* the chair (the projection of her experience on the earth), each emerging voice represented a particular aspect of her that had been formerly split off, held out of awareness. The experiment allowed her to observe these split-off parts that she projected onto the world. This was a world that sometimes would not (sadistically) or could not (helplessly) support her. The projected lack of support had felt so intolerable for her that she had been compelled to shut herself down and cut herself off from her own experience.

When overwhelming demands are made upon the infant or child at a time of development when she cannot cope, the consequent patterns of avoidance result in a loss of proprioceptive awareness. They become habitual and grow more fixed through time. The earlier in development that the experiences of such dangers and frustrations occur, the greater severity of disturbance.

To avoid experiencing her feelings of emptiness, every week Annie reported a watershed of dramatic events.

Everything seemed to be happening all at once, and yet, nothing much happened. During the session, whenever she moved closer to a feeling that was frightening to her, she seemed to experience some distracting physical discomfort. Thus, the drama continued.

In one particular session, Annie arrived appearing distraught, but when questioned, she was unsure of exactly what she was feeling. I asked her to turn her attention inward and to notice her experience. She closed her eyes, began to breathe, and reported a spasm in her back. Muscle spasms were an ongoing symptom for her and they exacerbated her constricted affect. "I can't get comfortable," she said with irritation. So I responded to what I postulated was a request for comfort. I asked her to lie over a large (eighty-five cm.) inflated gymnastic ball.

At this point, Annie and I had created a supportive enough relationship so that she could lie backward on the ball without feeling uncomfortably exposed. This trust had come from several years of my having been a consistent, available and predictable person in her life. Further, the ball offered her an increased surface of support which expanded her proprioception and allowed her to release her body weight. The taut extensor muscles of her back that she habitually used to hold herself up softened, and she reported feeling relaxed. From a background of reduced tension, Annie was able to sense minute changes in the whole of her experience.

I now instructed her to *push* both feet onto the floor which created a backward rocking motion, and to then *pull* the floor with her feet so that she could now rock herself forward. In full control of the rocking motion, her anxiety and excitement, often experienced in combination, were more supportable for her. She flexibly adjusted to the novelty of letting go. The subtle sensations of *falling* that had so terrified her when we first began our therapy, were now tolerated, even enjoyed. The elements of bending backward and balancing over the ball added lively sensations to the mix, and she was present.

As she arched over the ball, her upper chest opened and expanded. In this position, her routinely forced inhalations were interrupted, and she became more aware of her exhalations and better able to direct their slow, outward flow. The ball pushed up into her body and provided strong and comforting sensations. She melted into the ball and the ball melted into her.

During the ball experiments, Annie felt "joyous." She yearned, with every tissue of her body, for a harmony between herself and the world. When I watched her lie over the ball and breathe deeply, my body also relaxed and my breathing deepened. Annie and I were moving together. When she felt satisfied, Annie gently slid herself off the ball and onto the floor. Now seated, the sad and lonely feelings she had been holding at bay and out of her awareness were available to her.

So that she could sense the aftereffect of what had just occurred, these kinds of ball experiments were followed by Annie's standing. Upright, she was able to experience greater awareness of her body. Often, I guided her awareness with my hands and made slight adjustments to her posture. Sometimes I would shift the angle of her head, rotate her upper arm bones outward, or adjust her pelvis and ribs. These subtle alterations increased an awareness of each part of her body in relation to one another and the whole. They also produced immediate changes in her muscular constrictions, breathing rhythms, and, as she reported, her perceptions. Always I would have Annie stand and face me to experience our changing relationship. Most often, she felt open-hearted and close to me. I welcomed her.

Just as infants become aware of themselves through touching and moving, Annie was gaining a more lucid experience of herself. She was heightening her awareness of the incremental shifts in her muscular tensions. These were the somatic components of her *over-excitations* of panic/rage and her *under-excitations* of depression. At the same time, she became aware of the attitudes and beliefs that accompanied these postures. With a greater ability to influence her body, Annie began to experience a greater effectiveness in the world. She was learning to value all of her experiences.

Containing Emotions

The extent of Annie's justifiable terrors, marked by her constant vigilance, prevented her emotions from emerging naturally and spontaneously. Her tense body, inhibited breathing, and bound movement patterns could not provide a healthy container for her feelings. When her emotions emerged, she lacked the essential supports required to bear them, so she exploded with their energy into uncontrollable raging and crying.

During one session, Annie said she felt "uncomfortable" and promptly distracted herself by talking about something else. I told her that she was avoiding her feelings and could put them aside for the moment and with awareness, or learn to tolerate her discomfort. She chose the latter. To help support that process, I offered her a small rubber ball, five inches round. As she held it, I asked her to breathe, and with every exhalation to feel the weight of the ball contained within her hands. This accomplished, I asked her to feel the weight of the ball, to breathe and to feel the inside of her belly.

Once again, her focused attention to the ball's weight created a reduction of her overall hyper-muscularity. As her tension released, she was able to experience the more subtle sensations of her "insides." These were the feelings of emptiness that she routinely avoided by stuffing her belly with food and her mind with obsessive thinking. She became sad. She experienced a hopeless deprivation and loneliness. Now that she could breathe more easily and was able to contain her feelings, what had been impossible for her to bear became endurable. Her pain, the result of resisting whatever exists in the moment, gave way to surrender (to whatever exists) and eventually, it passed.

This ability to surrender to her discomforts was a prerequisite for the grief and mourning that would begin to move into the foreground. Until Annie was better supported internally, whenever her deep grief surfaced she would begin to cry. These cries soon moved into a kind of howling, interspersed with moments of raging or growling. Annie's body appeared convulsive: her toes, feet, and legs retracted into her trunk; her arms clutched the sides of her body; her hands grasped, her shoulders elevated; and her eyes slammed shut. Her head flopped laterally, alternating from side to side as if her neck muscles were insufficient to hold it in place. If not interrupted, this behavior could continue for a very long time. Annie was somewhere far off and was not coming back any time soon. As there was no awareness of self in her crying, she could never arrive at feeling consoled or satisfied. Empty of satisfaction, her howling cries returned again, suggesting the incompleteness of the process.

When an infant cries and reaches out for assistance, her breathing becomes irregular and her body tenses. When the caregiver responds, the infant's cries are comforted through holding and stroking, her deep breathing is restored, and her muscles relax once more. If the infant is not met in a satisfactory amount of time or in an appropriate way (this differs from one infant to another), crying develops into rage, exhaustion, and eventually despair.

My spontaneous response to Annie's bottomless cries was to take my hands and place them on her shoeless feet. I instructed, "Annie, feel my hands on your feet, and your feet on the ground. Cry and feel my hands, your feet, and the ground." Like a metronome setting a calm and steady rhythm, I repeated my words. "Annie, look at me. I'm here with you. Don't go so far away that I can't find you." Always, I would remind her to breathe.

Just as the gentle sound of the caregiver's voice stimulates receptors in the infant's inner ear and the baby is able to relax, my voice was calming to Annie. It was another way of subduing her overly active nervous system enough so that she could learn other, more satisfying modes of behaving. In these moments I wanted to give Annie *". . . as much support as necessary, as little as possible."* [3] This would enable her to access her own available but not yet fully developed resources. My presence and her increasing bodily awareness validated her experience, and she brought herself safely back into the moment.

Annie cried out for someone to console her. But the drama of her signaling left her out of touch with her own body and she was unable to hear whether anyone had answered her cry. During these sessions, I realized how deep her wounds were. I speculated these to be the unfinished experiences of early infancy and childhood, surfacing in the here and now. Annie's body was not a firm enough container to support her emotions and as a result her emotions were not fully defined or accessible to her. Her terror-driven cries reminded me of an early infant state, one that under better circumstances could refine into genuine emotions. The more defined the experience of body, the more refined the experience of emotions.

If Annie had been left to cry, a deeply familiar lack of support would have prevailed: she would have remained agitated, her feelings undifferentiated. Such unrefined emotions do not state the conditions of the field: Annie's relationship to whatever she was experiencing in the moment. This was a moment which included the air in the room, the ground under her feet, and me.

In the experience of emotions, we become aware of the appropriateness of our choices. They are *embodied knowing*. Without lucidity of emotion, Annie could not find relevant solutions to her dilemmas. She and I spent years working toward a verbal and movement vocabulary with which she could experience and express her emotions. In order for her to find it, the kinetic energy of her organ system had to be experienced, refined, and channeled through the coordination of her muscular and skeletal system.

Expressing Aggression

Often Annie would pull herself away from me in a siege of self-criticality or a harsh bout of self-hate. Once when I asked what was going on under her solemn, angry face, she replied, "I am taking a knife and slicing it into my abdomen and pulling it up to my neck." Several times the knife was pointed in my direction and I was sliced with great (imaginary) precision. At least her energy had moved outward.

Such compulsive fantasies, including sticking her head through a glass window, running her car into a wall, and slicing her abdomen and throat, were so compelling that they followed her into her dream life, where she was always running away from someone or something. Most often these "someones" were men with knives who were out to kill her. Unsupportable panic, terror, and helplessness were the companions of both her days and her nightmares. How could it have been otherwise for a child of incest who had to choose to comply with the confusions and disturbances of a stepfather offering her false solace in a desolate world?

There can be no healthy aggression when so much energy is turned inward. These self-inflicting fantasies were a perfect and oddly satisfying way for Annie to stay obsessively loyal to her family. The more compelling the fantasy, the deeper the loyalty. Most young children develop a healthy family loyalty. It is an aspect of loving. In families where the distress is great, loyalties are confused. When loyalty is the inability to separate from the other, relating becomes undifferentiated. The self is weakened and distorted.

For me to have had Annie *be* the knives and slash out would have been unsupported. To invite someone burdened with bitterness and rage to enact these feelings and become more bitter and raging can (like the crying) invite *disintegration*. The fuller realm of emotion cannot be supported by a body that is not fully experienced. Instead, I understood that Annie needed to experience *herself* while she was telling me with whom she was angry, and why. As she spoke, she was able to feel the support of her feet, hear the power of her voice, sense her breathing, *and* experience her angry excitements. Annie was present.

The experiments of becoming more in touch with her anger and the objects of it were painful for her. When she moved close to her hatred toward those early family members who had failed her, she swiftly backed away. With a heightened awareness of her behaviors and with greater sensorimotor supports in place, however, retreating from her aggression became less compelling and necessary for her. Her anger, like her crying, was supported, contained, and expressed.

Slowly, Annie became capable of expressing her hatred appropriately, and she began to see her husband more realistically. She realized that he could not give her what she had lost, nor what she perhaps never had. This was a stunning revelation for her, and she mourned. She learned that asking for something so unrealistic from her husband prevented her from getting anything from him at all, an unintended deprivation. In time, her relentless rages toward him became less frequent, and eventually they ceased.

Just as Annie was initially unable to support her grieving and lost herself to her rage, other more pleasurable feelings were thwarted. Whenever she was seen as worthy, or appreciated for who she was, she abruptly shut down. When she reported that someone had said something surprisingly kind or complimentary about her, she would hold her breath, lose the power of her voice, and look away from me. To experience feeling proud or gratified about herself would have breached the earlier loyalty. No one in her family had been allowed to feel good about him or herself except her blood brother, who had died young.

It was difficult for Annie to stay present when she told me about any compliment she had received. I asked her to feel her feet on the ground, lengthen her spine, breathe, and tell me her good news one word at a time. Only when she could locate the words someplace inside her body would she say them aloud. Sometimes repeating these words of praise sounded clumsy and felt unreal to her. At other times, she could sense the truth of her words, but lost the feeling when she looked at me. In time, she was able to risk talking about herself more positively, experience the pleasure in doing so, and directly share that feeling. Whenever she felt that I was with her, especially in the more snail-paced, moment-to-moment experiments, Annie would meet me most willingly. Through consistent, hard work, she gave up the false security of her self-hatred and her feelings of worthlessness. Annie, for those moments, allowed herself to be wonderful.

As she began to work through the complex and incestuous demands of her relationships with both stepbrother and stepfather, we could begin to address her eating dilemma. For many years she had been bulimic. Bulimia, an attempt to dispose of the background (early family) by throwing it up and out, contrasts with compulsive eating, which is an attempt to preserve the background. Although the bulimic symptom had ceased to exist at the time of our work, generalized confusion remained: what do I want to get rid of and what do I want to keep? The more Annie compulsively overate, the more she maintained an identity that was forged in her early upbringing: that of a worthless child. And, although the overeating filled her with self-loathing, it also afforded a familiar kind of comfort, support, and a ready supply of drama to her life.

One day, Annie and I were speaking of her relationship with chocolate. She was telling me how much she loved the sensations in her mouth, how creamy, how sweet. As she spoke, she brought her hand to her parted lips and gently stroked downward from her mouth to her throat, and toward her heart. She did this several times and with real gusto. I was taken with the obvious sensuality of her gesture and noticed my own developing hunger.

Although her lips were open and reaching as she gestured, I noted that her lower jaw was held in and back. I asked her to experiment by gliding her lower jaw forward and down as she reached with her mouth. When she found the coordination of the movement, I asked her to sense her lips, the inside of her mouth, and the root of her tongue. Suddenly, she startled. She had imagined herself in a desert, she said. She felt desperately parched, yet there was nothing to quench her thirst and no one to help her.

In the experiment, the habitual *holding* pattern, made most obvious by Annie's tense jaw as she reached with her mouth, loosened and disorganized. The release of muscular tension freed an emotional energy that was embedded within her habitual somatic pattern. Annie touched upon the terror of her empty existence, an omnipresent experience that was persistently pushed into the far background and well out of reach. To give up the eating rituals, her bingeing, she needed to enter this void: the *unfillable hole* that she was just coming to know in our sessions. The terror that she might cease to be was so dreadful that when a hint of it surfaced, Annie would go for the food. And although she clearly relished eating, she never really felt satisfied. A consistent nurturance was something she had not experienced in her early life. And she had yet to become this for herself.

During these early years of therapy, at session's end, Annie would ask, "Where's my cookie?" She wanted something to make her leaving more bearable. Although not all therapy sessions end in satisfaction or resolve, nor should they, I believed that Annie needed to leave with some offering from me. Rather than explore the request in depth, I would give her what she wanted, something that felt satisfying enough to her for the moment. This was the assurance that she had worked well in session and that something positive had come of it. When she could reassure herself, she stopped asking for that cookie. This took many years.

While the first five years of our working together were primarily focused on how Annie avoided her experiences by doing something to avert her anxiety, the next several years took on an added dimension. She was beginning to discover her resources. Her humor and intelligence were directed toward her new job and in several new friendships. She was easier with people, and the terrible feeling that everyone was out to get her diminished to a more manageable discomfort. Feeling safer, she felt free to be more spontaneous and she was recognized by others for her capabilities.

About three years into our therapy, Annie's husband was diagnosed with a terminal disease. She clearly told me that she was not ready to deal with his illness in therapy, and for some time we did not speak of it. Annie began to face the possibility of his death, however, when Vince was hospitalized and almost died.

With the prospect that Vince would die, her familiar grief and rage were brought to the surface. As is common to all those who live with someone who is terminally ill, Annie never knew if she should believe that Vince was going to die or that he might, somehow, survive. To stay with the unknown "I don't know what will happen" was intolerable for someone who had always been so devoted to controlling the inevitable. Annie had little tolerance for ambiguity. Now her life was being run by it.

During one of our sessions, she shared something with me that she had just read. "To deal with the death of a loved one," she recited, " . . . one has to do much more than just cope." I saw by the look on her face that she was preparing to more than cope with the tragedy of Vince's illness and his eventual death.

In the summer of 1993, Vince died at home in Annie's loving care. She was left alone. What often emerged in our therapy was a gentle flowing back and forth from her here and now experiences of loss to her losses early in life. Foreground related to background and Annie could more often contact the present. Now her feelings of deprivation, of being lost to or losing the other, were deeply experienced and expressed, and in those moments she moved into more healthy self.

Equally present were Annie's self-hatred and criticality. Still a seemingly reliable resource for her, they came forward with a vengeance after Vince's death. Her self-annihilation continued to be preferable to killing off the internalized, undesirable properties of those with whom she had for so long remained conflicted. This was, of course, her family of origin, who had left her abandoned and helpless.

Annie's self-hating often took the form of obsessive thinking about some personal or professional encounter that had gone wrong, or something at which she felt she had failed. She had frequent fantasies about smashing her head into a wall. During one session, when she was invested in this image of head-smashing, I built a stack of several wooden blocks (each block was nine inches long, five inches wide, and five inches high) and draped several well-folded blankets over them.[4] I asked Annie to stand in front of the pile (about two and one-half feet high) and to bend forward so that her head could rest upon it. This enabled both her head and feet to touch the *earth*.

I instructed her as to how to anchor her legs, where the weight of her body should fall, and where her head should touch the pile of blocks and blankets. I also told her to become aware of her exhale. (Inhaling is very difficult in the inverted posture.) Annie, now upside-down and with a different perspective on life, was busy attending to her body and her breathing. For these brief moments, she could not obsess.

The position heightened her awareness of her body-weight flowing downward and the concomitant response of the earth's upward force into her grounded head and lower limbs. When she reported feeling "well-supported" and could allow herself to yield, I instructed her to gently push her feet onto the earth, and to push her head onto the folded blankets. With every push, I asked her to repeat to herself, 'I am here.' Yielding in the vertical and inverted posture brought a balancing dimension to the experiment and improved her ability to orient, while pushing onto the floor with her feet and the blankets with her head illuminated the processes of differentiation—separating from, while including the other in experience.

When she came out of the position, the hypertonicity of her musculature was notably relaxed and she appeared calm. This was crucial for her, as she had lived a great deal of her life chronically overstimulated. Although some degree of arousal is important for the development of clear perceptions and emotions, in chronic hyper-arousal the person's experience of herself and the environment is obscured. Annie had felt vague and estranged most of her life. It was necessary to do whatever was possible to shift her experience, especially during these dramatic moments of self-hatred. Once she was calmed and available, we were able to explore the processes that led her to such self-torture. What had begun as an experiment of bodily processes *within* psychotherapy, was now converted to a relational experience *of* psychotherapy.

I created another experiment for Annie to help her experience her body and diminish her self-damaging, obsessive thinking. I had her stand with the front of her body facing a wall and asked her to bend forward, allowing her upper body to fold over the lower half. When she had done so, I asked her to bend her knees and adjust her position to the wall so that her upper spine touched the wall's surface. She stood in the posture for several minutes. The wall offered enough support so that her tightened spinal muscles could release. The pressure of the wall into her back also liberated the area of her front ribs and breastbone. She was free to breathe in this position and exhaled deeply. Stretching, her legs enlivened, and Annie said they felt "reliable." Her arms hung downward and pulled gently out of their sockets. She said that she could feel their full weight. She stood up and took a moment to sense herself. Her spine felt "free" and her limbs "alive," she repeated.

When an infant or child explores the environment without constraint, the spine develops flexibility and the limbs are free to contact the environment. If the surrounding environment inhibits freedom of expression, the spine stiffens or collapses, and the limbs lack a sense of aliveness. Whenever or wherever the flow of healthy aggressive energy is blocked, attention will not follow. The frustrated energy moves into fantasy and/or obsessive thinking.

Annie and I came to realize that when she was on the verge of change, her head-smashing fantasies would appear. They seemed to herald the event. Now she was relieved to have some awareness of how these fierce images functioned in her life. When they emerged in session, she would walk over to the wall and press her forehead on it, and breathe; then, like some violent storm, the torturing passed.

Through the use of our somatic/developmental experiments, the structural fixations that were blocking Annie's vital energy released. A reorganizing of her nervous system was made possible through a reorganizing of movement pattern. Annie contacted the present with the whole of her self.

Annie: 1996

Eleven years seems a long period of therapy. When a person has lived with great and early chaos, however, there are splits deeply embedded in the self, and coming into wholeness is an enormous challenge. It requires time, patience, and persistence. In our therapy together, Annie had changed enormously and at all levels of her existence.

Her spine had lengthened and her upper chest had softened and opened. Her bottom ribs released downward and were better aligned with her pelvis. Her neck softened, and the constrictions of her throat lessened. Her head, no longer pitched forward, was able to balance simply on her neck and torso. With a more mobile head, the sensory organs were better supported and her orienting skills were much improved.

The exaggerated arch of her low back had lessened such that Annie's legs were better placed in her hip sockets. She now had a more supple foundation for her pelvis and its contents, the abdominal and genital organs. The joints of her pelvis (sacrum and hip sockets) appeared more mobile, and there was more often a bounce to her stride. These areas, like the rest of her body, remained tense, but they were much less so than when we had begun our work.

Annie's breathing also had greater flexibility and adjusted more easily to new situations. When she was aware and breathed more deeply and evenly, she could either calm herself down or rise to the occasion. Although she was now far more willing to use her breath awareness as a resource, it was still difficult for her to draw upon it as a consistent support.

The improved somatic vocabulary vitalized her communicating skills. She became more secure in her ability to converse, and no longer needed a myriad dramatic facial expressions to signal her quickly changing moods and/or to comment negatively about herself and others.

Annie's somatic symptoms had also diminished considerably. She almost never reported the tensions in her back and neck; the pain along her breast-bone diminished; and the shakiness of her legs vanished. Although she experienced occasional tension in her jaw, it was minimal by comparison with her earlier pattern of clenching there. Exhaustion and collapse still occurred, but they did not continue for as long a period as earlier, nor were they as debilitating.

Annie still overate or binged. It was one of the remaining ways that she held fast to her familial loyalty. Her relationship with food provided a continual background dilemma, and it was difficult for her to let go of anything that remained constant. Eating also provided the comfort of being unconscious, which she felt she was not ready to give up. In all, however, even though difficulties remained, Annie was very much more her own person.

When she first came to therapy, she did not have the ability to recover from painful disturbances, whether perceived or actual. In the years we worked together, she made herself more flexible and considerably stronger. With this new resilience, she was able to recover from what she still perceived as threats to her existence—from a slight from an individual in whom she had vested power and authority—to the trauma of her husband's painful illness and death. During these episodes, Annie had fought hard to reorganize from a state of collapse. Each time, she came back from despair to fulfill more and more of her potential in the creating of a new self.

At one of our last sessions, Annie told me that she had written 260 pages of a novel in the last year. In the three years since Vince's death, she had also written several short stories, two children's stories, and some articles. One had been published.

At work, Annie had been invited to replace her supervisor. For a woman who could not easily concentrate on anything for more than a short period of time, was uneasy about relating to other people, and had problems with working well and consistently, this was a fine accomplishment.

In 1985, Annie had come to therapy greatly damaged and functioning poorly. With the inclusion of somatic and developmental movement patterns in our therapy, she was able to uncover and work through many of the blocks that had prevented her from feeling more whole and living life more fully. Now the present experience of her new self continually challenges her background identity of worthlessness. The conflict brings up anxiety for Annie, but it is an aware anxiety that is essential for her continuing maturation and that she is better able to support.

* * *

The crucial work of any therapy is to liberate the client's healthy aggression, the vital life force. If therapy is successful, the person is free to live a spontaneous and creative life. With fewer inhibitions in primary physiology, more and more areas of awareness can be assimilated into the background. The background now functions as the indispensable support for contacting.

Throughout our lifetimes, development continues through a process of organizing, disorganizing, and reorganizing movement patterns. These are the kinetic forces by which we change and grow. It is the work of the *self* at the cutting edge of experience.

This is the theory. This is the therapy.

Chapter Six Notes
Coming Into Wholeness: Annie's Story

1. In contraction, each of the muscle fibers composing an individual muscle takes turns working and resting (Juhan, 1987). If a muscle is contracted for a prolonged period of time, the rate of contraction and release of its various fibers increases. The shakiness may come from a rapid shifting of contraction and release in the fibers of the thigh muscles as they attempt to cut off the internal sensations of excitation.

2. Annie reported that she had been sexually violated by her step-father from the age of five until her early adolescence. In her teenage years, her stepbrother began an incestuous relationship with her.

3. Communication with Laura Perls, 1986.

4. Blocks and blankets are commonly used as "props" in the practice of Iyengar yoga. I have found them useful to the therapy session.

Resources For Therapists

Equipment Shop, Inc.
various size physioballs
P.O. Box 33, Bedford, MA 01730
781-275-7681   www.equipmentshop.com

Linda Tumbarello
various size physioballs
545 Riverside Drive, Florence, MA. 01062
413-586-5971

Tools for Yoga
blocks, blankets, sandbags, yoga mats
P.O. Box 99, Chatham, N. J. 07928
888-678-9642

Hugger-Mugger
blocks, blankets, sandbags, yoga mats
Salt Lake City, Utah 84123
800-473-4888   www.huggermugger.com

Sportime
physioballs and buddy/co-oper bands
One Sportime Way, Atlanta, GA. 30340-1402
800-850-8602   Fax 770-263-0897

Dye-namic Movement Products, Inc.
buddy/co-oper bands
33 Sloop Lane, Port Ludlow, WA. 98365
360-437-7733   www.dyenamicmovement.com

References

Alexander, R. and Boehme, R. (1993). *Normal Development of Functional Motor Skills: The First Year of Life.* Tucson: Therapy Skill Builders/The Psychological Corporation.

Ayers, J. (1955). Proprioceptive Facilitation Elicited through Upper Extremities. Part I, *American Journal of Occupational Therapy,* (Jan.-Feb.) 1-9.

Ayers, J. (1972). *Sensory Integration and Learning Disorders.* Los Angeles: Western Psychological Services.

Ayers, J. (1974). *The Development of Sensory Integrative Theory and Practice.* Dubuque, Iowa: Kendall/Hunt.

Ayers, J. (1979). *Sensory Integration and the Child.* Los Angeles: Western Psychological Services.

Bainbridge Cohen, B. (1993). *Sensing, Feeling and Action.* Northhampton, MA: Contact Editions.

Bartenieff, I. (1980). *Coping with the Environment.* New York: Gordon and Breach Science Publishers.

Bell, R. (1974). Contributions of Human Infants. In Lewis and Rosenblum (eds.), *The Effect of the Infant on its Caregivers.* New York: John Wiley and Sons.

Bly, L. (1983). *The Components of Normal Movement During the First Year of Life.* Chicago: The Neuro-Developmental Treatment Association.

Bly, L. (1994). *Motor Skills Acquisition in the First Year of Life*. Tucson: Therapy Skill Builders/The Psychological Corporation.

Bly, L. (1999). *Baby Treatment Based on NDT Principles*. Tucson: Therapy Skill Builders/The Psychological Corporation.

Boadella, R. (1987). *Lifestreams: An Introduction to Biosynthesis*. New York: Rutledge & Sons.

Bobath, K. and Bobath, B. (1965) . *Abnormal Postural Reflex Activity Caused by Brain Lesions*. London: William Heinemann Medical Books Ltd.

Brazelton, T., ed. (1990). *Touch: The Foundation of Experience*. Madison, CT: International Universities Press.

Brazelton, T. and Cramer, B. (1989). *The Earliest Relationship*. New York: Addison Wesley.

Bril, B. and Breniere, Y. (1989). Steady-State Velocity and Temporal Structure of Gait During the First Six Months of Autonomous Walking. *Human Movement Science* 8, 99-122.

Bushell, E. and Boudreau, P. (1993). Motor Development and the Mind: The Potential Role of Motor Abilities as a Determinant of Aspects of Perceptual Development. *Child Development* 64 (4), 1099-1110.

Camparetti, A. (1980). Pattern Analysis of Normal and Abnormal Development: The Fetus, the Newborn, the Child. *The Development of Movement in Infancy: Proceedings, May 18-24, School of Medicine, Department of Medical Allied Health Professionals.* North Carolina: University of North Carolina.

Crocker, S.F. (1999). *A Well Lived Life: Essays in Gestalt Therapy.* Boston: GIC Press.

Crutchfield, C. and Barnes, M. (1993). *Motor Control and Motor Learning in Rehabilitation.* Atlanta: Stokesville Publishing.

Deutsch, F. (1952). Analytic Posturology. *Psychoanalytic Quarterly 21,* 196-214.

Dowd, I. (revised ed. 1995). *Taking Root to Fly: Articles on Functional Anatomy.* New York: Contact Collaborations.

Feder, B. and Ronall, R., eds. (1996). *A Living Legacy of Fritz and Laura Perls: Contemporary Case Studies.* Montclair, NJ: Beefeeder Press.

Feldenkrais, M. (1949). *Body and Mature Behavior.* London: Routeledge and Kegan Paul.

Feldenkrais, M. (1981). *The Elusive Obvious.* Cupertino, CA: Meta Publications.

Feldenkrais, M. (1985). *The Potent Self.* CA: Harper & Row Publishing.

Fiorentino, M. (1981). *A Basis for Sensorimotor Development: Normal and Abnormal.* Springfield, IL: Charles C. Thomas.

Fogel, A. (1993). *Developing Through Relationships.* Chicago: University of Chicago Press.

Fraiberg, S. (1982). Pathological Defenses in Infancy. *Psychoanalytic Quarterly 51,* 612-635.

Fraiberg, S. (1987). *Selected Writings of Selma Fraiberg.* L. Fraiberg, ed., Columbus: Ohio State University Press.

Gesell, A. and Thompson, H. (1934). *Infant Behavior: Its Genesis and Growth.* New York: McGraw Hill.

Gibson, E. (1982). The Concept of Affordances in Development: The Renascence of Functionalism. In *The Concept of Development: Minnesota Symposium on Child Psychology, 15,* ed., W.A. Collins. Hillsdale, NJ: Lawrence Erlbaum.

Gibson, E. (1989). Exploratory Behavior in the Development of Perceiving, Acting, and Acquiring of Knowledge. *Annual Review of Psychology 39,* 1-41.

Gibson, J. (1962). Observations on Active Touch. *Psychological Review 69,* 491-499.

Gibson, J. (1979). *The Ecological Approach to Visual Perception.* Boston: Houghton Mifflin Company.

Goldstein, K. (1939). *The Organism.* Boston: Beacon Press.

Gorski, P. et al. (1990). Touch as an Integration and Learning System. In Brazelton (ed.) *Touch: The Foundation of Experience.* Madison, CT: International Universities Press.

Gottfried, A. (1990). Touch as an Organizer of Development and Learning. In Brazelton (ed.), *Touch: The Foundation of Experience.* Madison, CT: International Universities Press.

Harbourne, G. et al. (1993). A Kinematic and Electromyographic Analysis of the Development of Sitting Posture in Infants. *Developmental Psychobiology* 26, 51-64.

Hartley, L. (1994). *Wisdom of the Body Moving.* Berkeley, CA: North Atlantic Books.

Juhan, D. (1987). *Job's Body.* New York: Station Hill Press.

Kalverboer, et al. (1993). *Motor Development in Early and Later Childhood.* Great Britain: Cambridge University Press.

Keleman, S. (1985). *Emotional Anatomy.* Berkeley, CA: Center Press.

Kephart, N. and Chaney, C. (1968). *Motoric Aids to Perceptual Training.* Columbus, OH: Charles Merrill Publishing.

Kepner, J. (1987). B*ody Process: A Gestalt Approach to Working with the Body in Psychotherapy.* Boston: GIC Press.

Kestenberg, J. (1965). The Role of Movement Patterns in Development: I Rhythms of Movement. *Psychoanalytic Quarterly 34*, 1-36.

Kestenberg, J. (1965). The Role of Movement Patterns in Development: II Flow of Tension and Effort. *Psychoanalytic Quarterly 34*, 517-563.

Kestenberg, J. (1967). The Role of Movement Patterns in Development: III The Control of Shape. *Psychoanalytic Quarterly 36*, 356-409.

Kitzler, R. (1998). *The Bases of Gestalt Therapy: An Evolutionary Restatement.* As yet unpublished paper, New York Institute for Gestalt Therapy.

Korner, A. (1990). The Many Faces of Touch. In Brazelton, T. (ed.), *Touch: The Foundation of Experience.* Madison, CT: International Universities Press.

Kruger, D. (1989). *Body Self and Psychological Self.* New York: Bruner Mazel.

Kuo, Z. (1967). *The Dynamics of Behavior and Development: An Epigenetic View.* New York: Random House.

Lay, J. (1997). *On the Nature of Gestalt Therapy.* As yet unpublished paper, New York Institute for Gestalt Therapy.

Lee, A. (1974). Visual Perceptive Control of Standing in Human Infants. *Perception and Psychophysics 15*, 529-532.

Lichtenberg, J. (1983). *Psychoanalysis and Infant Research.* Hillsdale, NJ: Lawrence Erlbaum Associates.

Lichtenberg, P. (1969). *Psychoanalysis: Conservative and Radical.* New York: Springer Publishing Inc.

Lichtenberg, P. (1996). *Remembering Isadore's Gestalt Therapy.* As yet unpublished paper, Philadelphia, PA.

Latner, J. (1986). *The Gestalt Therapy Book.* New York: The Center for Gestalt Development, Inc.

Lowen, A. (1958). *Physical Dynamics of Character Structure.* New York: Grune and Stratton.

Marcher, L. (1996). *The Body Self in Psychotherapy: A Psychomotor Approach to Self-Psychology.* As yet unpublished paper, Biodynamic Institute.

Meade, V. (1998). *Partners in Movement: A Family-Centered Approach to Pediatric Kinesiology.* San Antonio: Therapy Skill Builders/The Psychological Corporation.

Merleau, P. (1962). *The Phenomenology of Perception.* New York: Humanities Press.

Meltzoff, A. and Borton, R.W. (1979). Intermodal Matching by Human Neonates. *Nature 282,* 403-404.

McGraw, M. (1945). *The Neuromuscular Maturation of the Human Infant.* New York: Columbia University Press.

Neisser, U. ed. (1993). *The Perceived Self.* New York: Press Syndicate: University of Cambridge.

Perls, F., Hefferline, R., and Goodman, P. (1951). *Gestalt Therapy: Excitement and Growth in the Human Personality.* New York: Julian Press.

Perls, L. (1993). *Living at the Boundary.* New York: Gestalt Journal Press.

Polster, E. and Polster, M. (2000). *From the Radical Center: The Heart of Gestalt Therapy.* Boston: GIC Press.

Prechtl, H. (1993). Principles of Early Motor Development in the Human. In Kalverboer (ed.), *Motor Development in Early and Later Childhood.* Great Britain: University Press.

Randolph, S. and Heiniger, M. (1994). *Kids Learn from the Inside Out.* Boise, ID: Legendary Publishing.

Reese, M. (fall/winter 1999/2000). A Dynamic Systems View of the Feldenkrais Method. *Somatics 12*, 3, 18-26.

Reich, W. (1949). *Character Analysis.* New York: Orgone Institute Press.

Rouchat, P. and Goubet, N. (1995). Development of Sitting Reaching in Five to Six Month-Old Infants. *Infant Behavior and Development* 18, 53-68.

Schilder, P. (1947). *Mind: Perception and Thought in Their Constructive Aspects.* New York: Columbia University Press.

Schilder, P. (1950). *The Image and Appearance of the Human Body.* New York: International Universities Press.

Schilder, P. (1964). *Contributions to Developmental Neuro-psychiatry* New York: International Universities Press.

Schore, A. (1994). *Affect Regulation and the Origin of the Self.* Hillsdale, NJ: Lawrence Erlbaum.

Smith, E.W.L. (1985). *The Body in Psychotherapy.* North Carolina/London: McFarland & Company, Inc.

Spitz, R. (1959). *A Genetic Field Theory of Ego Formation.* New York: International Universities Press.

Sporns, O. and Edelman, G. (1993). Solving Bernstein's Problem: A Proposal for the Development of Coordinated Movement by Selection. *Child Development 64,* 960-981.

Stern, D. (1974). Mother and Infant at Play. In Lewis and Rosenblum (eds.), *The Effect of the Infant on Its Caregivers.* New York: John Wiley and Sons.

Stern, D. (1977). *The First Relationship.* Cambridge, MA: University Press.

Stern, D. (1985). *The Interpersonal World of the Human Infant.* New York: Basic Books.

Stoehr, T. (1994). *Here, Now, Next: Paul Goodman and the Origins of Gestalt Therapy.* Boston: GIC Press.

Swinnen, S. et al. (1994). *The Interlimb Coordination: Neural, Dynamical, and Cognitive Constraints.* CA: Academic Press.

Thelen, E. (1989). Self Organization in Developmental Processes: Can Systems Approaches Work?, *Minnesota Symposia on Child Psychology 22*, 77-117.

Thelen, E. (1992). Development as a Dynamic System. *Current Directions in Psychological Science 1*, 189-193.

Thelen, E. (1995). Motor Development: A New Synthesis. *American Psychologist – Journal of the American Psychological Association 50*, 2.

Thelen, E. and Smith, L. (1993). *A Dynamic Systems Approach to the Development of Cognition and Action.* Cambridge, MA: MIT Press: Bradford Book Series in Cognitive Psychology.

Thelen, E. et al. (1984). The Relationship between Physical Growth and a Newborn Reflex. *Infant Behavior and Development 7*, 479-493.

Thelen, E. et al. (1987). Self-Organization of Emotional Development. *Psychoanalytic Inquiry 1*, 189-193.

Thelen, E. et al. (1987). Self-Organizing Systems and Infant Motor Development. *Developmental Review 7*, 39- 65.

Thelen, E. et al. (1993). The Transition to Reaching: Mapping Intention and Intrinsic Dynamics. *Child Development 64*, 4, 1058-1098.

Todd, M. (1937). *The Thinking Body.* New York: Paul B. Hoeber, Inc.

Trevarthen, C. (1977). Descriptive Analysis of Infant Communication Behavior. In H.R. Schaffer (ed.), *Studies in Infant-Mother Interaction.* London: Academic Press.

Trevarthen, C. (1986). Form, Significance and Pscyhological Potential of Hand Gestures in Infants. In Nespoulous, A. et al. (eds.), *The Foundations of Gestures: Motor and Semiotic Aspects.* Hillsdale, NJ: Lawrence Erlbaum.

Wheeler, G. (1991). *Gestalt Reconsidered: A New Approach to Contact and Resistance.* Boston: GIC Press.

Wheeler, G. (2000). *Beyond Individualism: Toward a New Understanding of Self, Relationship, and Experience.* Boston: GIC Press.

Winnicott, D.W. (1964). *The Child, the Family, and the Outside World.* New York: Addison-Wesley.

Woolacott, M. and Shumway-Cook, A. eds. (1990). *The Development of Posture and Gait Across the Lifespan.* South Carolina: University of South Carolina Press.

Yontef, G. (1993). *Awareness Dialogue and Process: Essays on Gestalt Therapy.* New York: The Gestalt Journal Press

Index

A

aggression, 201–203
alienation, 69, 70
anxiety, chronic, alignment of
    units of weight in, 76
autonomy
    infants and, 41
    movement patterns and, 40
avoidance, 193, 194
awareness, 70, 106, 192
    of body weight, 71, 72

B

body/environment relationship,
    70
body-weight experience, 75, 81,
    82
    and orienting processes, 72
    and postural types, 73
    developmental movement
    patterns and, 76–77
    in clients, 78–79
    infant/caregiver relationship
    and, 77–78
bulimia, 204

C

center of gravity, 75, 76
client, posture and movements
    of, 22–23, 56–57, 88–89,
    95–97, 116–117, 123–124,
    152–154, 166–168,
    180–184, 211–212
client/therapist relationship, 39,
    47, 53, 179–180, 184–192
    reaching in, 106
contacting, 70, 72, 179

and differentiation, 42, 46, 53
definition of, 41–42
disturbances of, 115
evaluation of during
    therapy, 54
supports for, 46, 51, 53
crawling, 43

D

depression
    alignment of units of weight
    in, 75–76
    postural pattern in, 73–74
developmental body-language,
    21
developmental movement
    patterns, 79
    and body weight experience,
    76–77
    and differentiation, 40–41
    as self-organized, 43
    assimilation of, 46, 51
    discordant, 48
    disorganization of, 43, 51
    emerging, 42, 144
    in overlapping sequences, 45
    integration of earlier, 43–44,
    45
developmental theory, movement
    patterns and, 40
differentiation, 46, 64, 65, 141
    in adults, 53
    in infants, 50, 63
    of body parts, 146, 147, 148,
    149
    role of developmental move-
    ment patterns in, 40–41